Anonymous

Three Dedications

Soldier's Monument at South Sutton, Pillsbury FreeLibrary at Warner, Margaret Pillsbury General Hospital at Concord, 1891

Anonymous

Three Dedications

Soldier's Monument at South Sutton, Pillsbury FreeLibrary at Warner, Margaret Pillsbury General Hospital at Concord, 1891

ISBN/EAN: 9783744669511

Printed in Europe, USA, Canada, Australia, Japan

Cover: Foto ©ninafisch / pixelio.de

More available books at **www.hansebooks.com**

THREE DEDICATIONS.

SOLDIERS' MONUMENT
AT SOUTH SUTTON.

PILLSBURY FREE LIBRARY
AT WARNER.

MARGARET PILLSBURY GENERAL HOSPITAL
AT CONCORD.

1891

Concord, N. H.:
Republican Press Association, Railroad Square.
1891.

PREFACE.

Three unparalleled events occurred in New Hampshire within a month, in the autumn of 1891. These were the dedication of the Monument to commemorate the patriotism of the loyal men of Sutton who fell in the War of the Rebellion, of a Free Public Library for the intellectual culture and literary entertainment of the people of Warner and all sojourners therein, and of a General Hospital for the care of sick and disabled persons in the city of Concord. All these were the outgrowth of the well matured plans and munificence of a native of the first named town, and a resident in the prime of life of the last named town and city. It is most desirable that the exercises upon those occasions should be put in a more enduring form than in the columns of a newspaper or the pages of a pamphlet. With this end in view, this volume has been prepared and published, to be placed where it can be conveniently referred to for all coming time.

GEORGE ALFRED PILLSBURY.

GEORGE ALFRED PILLSBURY is the second son of Captain John and Susanna (Wadleigh) Pillsbury, and was born in Sutton, August 29, 1816. He is of the sixth generation of descendants of William Pillsbury, the common ancestor of the Pillsbury families of this country, who came from Essex county, England, in 1640, to Dorchester, Mass., where he married Dorothy Crosby, and in 1651 removed to Newbury, Mass. (now a part of Newburyport), in which city a third meeting of the Pillsbury descendants was held on the 3d of September last.

Mr. Pillsbury received a good common-school education, and at the age of eighteen went to Boston, where he found employment in the grocery and fruit store of Job Davis, a native of Sutton, then doing business under Boylston Market. He remained in Boston a little over a year, when he returned to Sutton and engaged in the manufacture of stoves and sheet-iron ware—an industry then in its infancy in this state—with his cousin, John C. Pillsbury. He continued in this business for several years. On February 1, 1840, he embarked in mercantile life as a clerk in the store of John H. Pearson, in Warner, and in July following he purchased the business, and conducted it successfully for nearly eight years, alone or in partnership. In the spring of 1848 he went into a wholesale dry goods house in Boston, where he remained for a year. In 1849 he returned to Warner, where he again opened a store, which he conducted until 1851, when he sold out his business and removed to Concord. During his residence in Warner he served as selectman and treasurer, represented the town in the legislature in 1850–'51, and was postmaster from 1844 to 1849.

In 1851 the county convention of representatives in the legislature decided to build a new jail for Merrimack county. Mr. Pillsbury was made one of the committee to select a site for it, and he was authorized to superintend its construction, which he did,—the jail being completed in the spring of 1852. In December, 1851, he began his duties as purchasing agent of the Concord Railroad, and continued the same without interruption until July, 1875, a period of nearly twenty-four years. He was one of the organizers and directors of the First National Bank in 1864, was elected its president in 1866, and continued to hold that office until his removal from the state twelve years later. He was also one of the organizers of the National Savings Bank, and its first president, which position he held from 1867 to 1874. He served in the board of aldermen from Ward Five in 1873 and 1874, as representative in the legislature from the same ward in 1871 and 1872, and as one of the committee of three, in 1876, to appraise all the real estate in Concord for purposes of taxation. He was elected mayor of the city in 1876, and reëlected in 1877. During his residence in Concord he was active in all enterprises for the improvement and welfare of the city, and was a generous contributor to benevolent and charitable objects. He served as one of the building committee of the high-school edifice in 1863; as one of the trustees of the Centennial Home for the Aged, to the starting of which he contributed liberally; and was also trustee of the State Orphans' Home on the Webster farm in Franklin, which position he held until his removal from the state. The bell above the dome on the Board of Trade building was a gift from him to the city of Concord, and the fine organ in the First Baptist church was the joint gift of himself and his son, Hon. Charles A. Pillsbury.

When Mr. Pillsbury removed from Concord to Minneapolis, in March, 1878, complimentary resolutions were passed unanimously by the city council, the directors of the First National Bank, the First Baptist church and society, and the Webster Club; and a similar testimonial, signed by more than three hundred of the leading citizens, representing all classes of business men and professions, was presented to him.

Mr. Pillsbury's life in the North-west has been no less active than it was in the East. As a member of the firm of Charles A. Pillsbury & Co., the largest flouring firm in the world, it would seem as though he might have found ample employment for his time. But in his new home other honors awaited him. He was elected mayor of Minneapolis, in 1884, for two years, and during his administration the first paving was done in the streets of that city, and other marked improvements begun and carried forward. He has served as president of the City Council, the Minneapolis Board of Trade, the Chamber of Commerce, the Homœopathic Hospital and the Minneapolis Free Dispensary, the Board of Water-Works, the Pillsbury & Hurlbert Elevator Co., the St. Paul and Minneapolis Baptist Union, the Minnesota Baptist State Convention, and the American Baptist Missionary Union; as vice-president of the Minnesota Loan and Trust Co.; as president of the North-Western National Bank; as director of the Manufacturers' National Bank and the Minneapolis Elevator Co.; as a member of the School Board and of the Board of Park Commissioners; and held trusteeships in many other organizations.

In 1885 he was chairman of the committee to build the First Baptist church—a model modern church edifice in all its appointments, and the largest and finest church west of Chicago, costing about $150,000. Its organ is the best in the city, and was a gift from Mr. and Mrs. Pillsbury, and their sons, Charles A. and Fred C. Pillsbury. Before leaving New Hampshire, Mr. Pillsbury contributed liberally to Colby academy at New London; and since he located in Minneapolis he has given two buildings—one a ladies' boarding hall and the other an academy building—to the Pillsbury academy at Owatonna, Minnesota, erected in 1886 and in 1889 respectively, at an expense of $75,000.

During the past year Mr. Pillsbury has given much time to supervising the plans and the work of erecting the several structures recently dedicated at Sutton, Warner, and Concord, making several journeys East in that time. Although he has passed by several years the Psalmist's lease of life, he is the possessor of good health, and surrounded by all the comforts of an elegant home; and, receiving the tender and watchful care of a devoted wife and children, and the respect of all who know him, the evening of his life is passing beautifully and peacefully, in one of the most wonderful cities of the wonderful North-west.

MARGARET CARLETON PILLSBURY.

MARGARET SPRAGUE CARLETON was the third daughter and fifth child of Henry and Polly (Greeley) Carleton, of Sutton, who removed to Bucksport, Me., soon after their marriage, and where Margaret S. was born, September 20, 1817. In 1823 her father's family returned to Sutton, and there she received her education in the common schools. On May 9, 1841, she was united in marriage to George A. Pillsbury, then in trade in Warner, and removed to that town and began housekeeping, as was the good old New England custom in those days. From that day to the present time she has been his helpmeet indeed, and the sharer of all his joys and sorrows. Possessed of great kindness of heart, her sympathy has gone out to the needy and suffering, and her strict conscientiousness and sincere friendship have caused her counsel to be sought, her judgment valued, and her influence strongly felt, in all matters of church or society wherever she has lived. She has ever sought to make her home attractive and happy, and the best tribute that an appreciative and loving husband could pay to her devotion and fidelity as wife and mother was the giving of her name to an elegant hospital building, erected for the care and comfort of the sick and suffering. Of three children born to them, two survive to honor their father and mother—Charles A. and Fred C. Pillsbury.

SOLDIERS' MONUMENT,

SUTTON, NEW HAMPSHIRE.

On the plinth in raised letters is inscribed,—

> A GIFT TO THE TOWN
> OF SUTTON FROM
> GEORGE ALFRED PILLSBURY
> WHO WAS BORN NEAR THIS SPOT
> A. D. 1816.

The monument is surrounded with a granite curbing twenty-five feet square, taken from King's Hill quarry in Sutton. The monument was designed, made, and erected by Charles E. Cummings, of Nashua, a native of Sutton. It is of beautiful design and excellent workmanship.

DEDICATORY EXERCISES.

The dedication of the soldiers' monument at South Sutton occurred on Tuesday, September 1, 1891. The exercises were under the direction of Robert Campbell Post, No. 58, G. A. R., and the dedicatory ceremonies were performed by officers of the New Hampshire department of the Grand Army of the Republic. A procession was formed in the following order:

Chief marshal, Colonel Timothy B. Lewis.
Aids, Captain George Robinson, G. T. Dunfield.
Manchester War Veterans' Drum Corps, D. H. Bean, leader.
Company A, Third Regiment, N. H. N. G., New London, Captain Baxter Gay.
Manchester Drum Corps.
W. W. Brown Camp, No. 1, S. V., Manchester, Commander West.

Robert Campbell Post. No. 58, G. A. R., Sutton, Commander Edwin Lear.

Bradford Cornet Band, E. G. Hoyt, leader.

Mason W. Tappan Camp, S. V., Bradford, Commander Will Pressey.

Anthony Colby Post, G. A. R., No. 85, New London, John K. Law, commander.

New London Cornet Band, Fred Goings, leader.

Prescott Jones Post, No. 32, G. A. R., Wilmot, B. S. Kenison, commander.

Delegates from Senator Grimes Post, No. 25, G. A. R., Hillsborough, John Booth, commander.

Department Commander Everett B. Huse, G. A. R., Acting Senior Vice Commander Frank G. Noyes, Junior Vice Commander A. J. Sanborn, Acting Chaplain A. C. Hardy, Assistant Adjutant-General James Minot, and Medical Director Royal B. Prescott, M. D., of Nashua, and Philip C. Bean, A. D. C., of Concord, of Commander Huse's staff.

Invited guests.

At 12 o'clock m. the procession moved to a large tent near by, in which plates had been laid for three hundred persons, and a bountiful dinner was served, which was provided by the ladies of the town and the comrades of the post living in adjoining towns.

Among the guests and prominent persons present were Hon. George A. Pillsbury and wife, and daughter, Mrs. Townsend, ex-Governor John S. Pillsbury and wife, and F. A. Fisher, of Minneapolis; General John Eaton, orator of the day, his brother, Hon. Lucius B. Eaton, of Memphis, Tenn., and the latter's son, Valentine W. Eaton, a member of Dartmouth college; Rev. William S.

Palmer, D. D., of St. Louis, Mo.; Charles E. Cummings, architect and builder of the monument, of Nashua; Mrs. Augusta Harvey Worthen, of Lynn, Mass., historian of the town, and her nephew, Charles H. Kohlrausch, Jr., of Billerica, Mass.; John A. Andrews and wife, of Boston, the latter a daughter of the late Hon. Owen Lovejoy, of Illinois; Colonel H. B. Titus, of New York city; Rev. J. C. Ager, of Brooklyn, N. Y.; General Luther McCutchins and General J. M. Clough, of New London; ex-Governor N. G. Ordway, of Dakota; Major Samuel Davis, Albert P. Davis, Esq., Robert Thompson, Ira Harvey and wife, of Warner; H. G. Carleton, of Newport; Thomas W. Pillsbury and Colonel L. H. Carroll, of Concord.

The procession re-formed soon after dinner had been served, and escorted the guests and others to the stand near the monument, where the exercises took place. At 1 o'clock p. m., S. N. Welch, M. D., president of the day, called the assembly to order, and Rev. J. D. Waldron, of Springvale, Me., offered a fervent prayer. Ephraim Bean, chairman of the board of selectmen, made the following address of welcome:

FELLOW-CITIZENS OF SUTTON: I am happy to meet so many here on this occasion. Probably there has not been an event, from the earliest history of our town until the present time, that our people have looked forward to with more pleasant anticipations than the dedication of this beautiful monument, or one in which they have felt so deep an interest. You have shown this by the prompt contribution from your treasury, and by the many willing workers giving time and personal means freely that this day should be successful, and should last as a pleasant memory. Therefore I feel that I but echo the voice of my towns-people when I bid you welcome. And so, ladies and gentlemen, I bid you a hearty welcome to our town to-day, and thank you for your presence, and for the interest you have taken in these exercises.

I see before me a large delegation of the Grand Army of the Republic and of the Sons of Veterans. You do our town an honor by your presence here to-day. This beautiful shaft of granite has been erected to perpetuate the memory of the men who went from Sutton to fight, in the War of the Rebellion, for the protection of the Union. May it be as lasting as our grand, beloved hills, and, like them, point our aspirations to better deeds. You not only honor Sutton, but you honor every man who went to the war from our town, and in their behalf I especially thank you for your presence on this occasion.

We have another class with us to-day that are always welcome—these invited guests and former residents of our town. Many of you I have known in other years, when you moved in our society. Memory recalls the days of long ago, when we bathed in these beautiful lakes and roamed over these beautiful hills. Gentlemen, we have watched you with deep interest. When you have prospered in business, we have rejoiced with you. When you have been honored with offices of trust, the gifts of

the people, we have been proud that you were
natives of our town. But, ladies and gentlemen,
probably there has never been any other name, of
those who went out from our town, so generally
known as that of the two brothers who are here
with us to-day. It is not only known all over
the United States, but in the Dominion of Canada,
Mexico, the South American states, the countries of
Europe, and all other foreign nations. Their name
has been stamped upon barrels of flour, and scattered like leaves by the winds of autumn. Their
immense business is too well known to us all for
any words of mine to be of interest; its magnitude
may be judged by the fact that one of them is
known as "The Flour King of the World."

And now, ladies and gentlemen, I not only have
the pleasure, but the honor, of introducing to you
one of these brothers, the Hon. George A. Pillsbury, of Minneapolis, who will now address you.

MR. PILLSBURY'S ADDRESS.

I stand to-day within sight of the place where
seventy-five years ago last Saturday I was born.
After remaining here for a little more than twenty-
three years, I left the good old town of Sutton and
took up my residence elsewhere. I can truthfully
say that I have never been ashamed to have it
known that I was a native of the old Granite State,
and was born in Sutton. More than half a century
has passed, and many events have transpired since
I left my native home yonder, and, although other
faces and other scenes have engrossed my time and

THE NEW YORK
PUBLIC LIBRARY

ASTOR, LENOX AND
TILDEN FOUNDATIONS
R   L

attention, still there is no spot more familiar to my eyes or more sacred to my heart than this little village of South Sutton. As I stand here and look into the faces of this generous company, another panorama than the faces and forms of those present passes before me—faces and forms which I shall never see again in this world. All that home and father and mother, and childhood and youth and young manhood, with all that their tender and vivid recollections imply, comes to me now. My mind reverts to my school-boy days, when the boys and girls of the families of the Savorys, the Blakes, the Carletons, the Thissels, the Dodges, the Peaslees, the Robys, the Dressers, the Littlehales, the Champlains, the Putneys, the Philbrooks, and others to the number of about one hundred, went to the old school-house which stood on the same spot as the one yonder. There was where most of us secured what education we ever had. Perhaps I was a little more fortunate than most of my other schoolmates, as I was allowed to attend a private school for ten weeks; and this completed all the school privileges I have ever been permitted to enjoy. I forget the cares and the business of the intervening half century which has elapsed since I bade good-bye to this place, and I see again the old scenes and live over the old memories. Far easier would it be for me, rather than to attempt to speak to you publicly, to converse with you privately, and live over again in thought and reminiscence the days when I was one of you. Although other places have been my home, and business elsewhere has taken my attention, yet there are no people dearer to me than those of the old south village. And as the advancing years come, the tendency of human nature to dwell upon scenes of childhood and youth will still more emphasize and deepen my love for this place.

And there, too, attended, in that same schoolhouse yonder, Margaret S. Carleton, who afterwards became my life's partner, and with whom I recently celebrated the golden anniversary of our wedding,—my wife, who in all the experiences of my life has ever shared with me its trials as well as its joys, and by her words and her presence has ever contributed to my success and happiness; and to-day she joins me in this gift to the home of our youth.

Had I the time, and were this the occasion, I would like to add my tribute to that hardy race of pioneers who peopled this community, and who, although they have passed away, have by their sturdy character and mental vigor left descendants of whom any town might be proud. And I often think, when we Americans boast of the tremendous development which our country has had in the Central, Western, and North-Western states during the past fifty years, that we neglect to give credit to the real source and cause of our great growth and prosperity. It has been said that the principal product of New Hampshire has been men—a more important fruitage than any product of the soil, or of any industry or business pursuit. Sutton has been the nursery of many strong men. It is the virtue wrapt up in the seed which determines what the future plant will be. The hardy character, mental vigor, thrift, economy, and intelligence which are characteristic of the minds of those who have been reared in this town, and who have gone forth to many distant points, have produced results which are really the property and heritage of this place. Unfortunately, the superficial observer does not realize the heritage that belongs to a place like this. In measuring Sutton, we should not look alone at what we see here to-day, although we have reason to be proud of this, but we should go back and trace the lines and careers which radiate from this place into the different parts of our country, and consider all that these have accomplished. While I would not underrate the West, yet in a sense it is true that the West has been the receptacle of what has grown out of the East. The producing cause has been here; and while we cannot take the oak and crowd it back into the acorn again, yet we must remember that there is nothing in the oak which did not exist in the acorn, and that the soil which produced the acorn is really the mother of the oak. The winds and circumstances have merely transported the acorn from the soil where it was formed. Our debt of gratitude to-day should be to our ancestors,—among whom were the Harveys, Wadleighs, Eatons, Keazers, Kimballs, Andrews, Nelsons, Littles, Blaisdells, Johnsons, Pages, Beans, and many of the other old families of this town,— many of whose descendants are before me to-day, and from whom have sprung a strong, sturdy race of people. I venture the assertion that no town in the state, of the same number of inhabitants, can boast of a more intelligent, honest, honorable constituency. None has been more free from crime of all sorts; none has contributed more to the support of its common schools; none has done more for the elevation of its people.

Although Sutton is an agricultural town, and without the aid of railroads and many of the modern advantages, yet her sons and daughters have always shown courage, patriotism, and character. They have always met their financial obligations. The war debt, which hangs over many towns and cities in this country, has been paid off in Sutton. She is entirely free from debt, and has money in the treasury. But not only in money did this town do its duty in the War of the Rebellion, but she responded with what is more valuable, namely, human courage and human life. Little do most of us appreciate the sacrifice, the patriotism, and the devotion to the cause of free government made by those who, at the first assault on the integrity of the best government ever devised by man, sprang at once to arms and volunteered their services, in order that this government might be maintained and perpetuated.

This attempt to disrupt and destroy our government resulted in the greatest war the world has ever witnessed. During its continuance it is estimated that more than two millions of men were called upon to subdue it by force of arms. It is also estimated that at least one million of these men were either killed in battle, starved to death in rebel prisons, or have died since the war as the result of wounds received in battle. Nearly all the great leaders of the war have died before their time, and the rank and file are dropping off rapidly in consequence of exposures endured during their time of service.

Let us for the moment go back to the years of 1861 to 1865. See those stalwart, patriotic young men, in the prime of life, who are about to respond to the call of their country! See those fathers, mothers, brothers, sisters, sweethearts, whose hearts are being wrung with anguish and whose eyes are bathed in tears at the idea of giving up their dear ones to go to war, with the chances against their ever seeing them again! See those mothers, wives, and dear ones during the progress of that cruel war, waiting with intense eagerness to hear the result of battle after battle! How anxiously they visit the post-office, and seek all other avenues of information, in order to ascertain the fate of their dear ones! See those little ones gathered about the knee of their mother, watching with deepest feeling the emotions kindled in her countenance as she reads the last letter or intelligence from the father! See also those family groups, listening with bated breath to learn whether they have been made widows and orphans! Hear the wails of woe that go up from those family circles, as the sad intelligence is brought to them that their dear ones have fallen in battle on a far distant field!

When we consider all these matters, we are in part only prepared to realize what these sacrifices cost; and I have thought that I could bestow no more worthy testimonial of my love for my native place than to cause to be erected on this spot this soldiers' monument, in commemoration of the valor and courage of those men who, in the hour of their country's need, took their lives in their hands to uphold and preserve our national heritage. I believe Sutton is credited with having furnished over one hundred and fifty soldiers during the late struggle; and I would have this monument commemorate not only the valor of those brave men who responded to their country's need, but I would have it represent the courage and the patriotism which prompted this response in their hearts, and also represent the love and patriotism of those mothers, wives, and sisters who surrendered their dearest gifts—their sons, husbands, and brothers—to their country. Had I time, I would like to speak of Hiram K. Little, and others, who showed a bravery equal to that of any of our Revolutionary heroes.

And not only in the War of the Rebellion did Sutton send forth her brave soldiers, but ever since the settlement of the town, in 1767, Sutton has been represented in times of war with her full quota of soldiers. In the French and Revolutionary wars, in the War of 1812, and in the Mexican War she responded to duty's call. Prior to the year 1800, at least thirty-five men served in the French and Revolutionary wars, and about forty shared in the War of 1812; and I would, by this monument, ever keep alive the bravery of these men too.

To you, gentlemen, who represent the people of Sutton, and to your successors in office, I present this monument—to the citizens of this town and to those who shall follow us. Many of us have passed the summit of life, and are going down the declivity on the other side. The sunset of life is fast approaching. Other generations will soon follow us; and it is my hope that this monument may in some measure serve not only to keep alive the names of the muster-roll of Sutton, but also place beyond forgetfulness the qualities of those persons and those families which have been preserved in print by Augusta Harvey Worthen and Erastus Wadleigh, in their exceedingly valuable and carefully prepared history of this town. I thank God that He has spared my life until the present time, and that He has put into my hands sufficient means to enable me to pay this tribute of love and affection to the people of my native town, and also that He has enabled me to repay in part that debt of gratitude which we all owe to the noble men, dead and alive, who made these sacrifices that we may continue to enjoy the benefits and blessings of our dearly beloved country.

I would have not only the boys and girls of this town of to-day, and those who shall come after them, look to this shaft, ever pointing heavenward, for inspiration, but I would also have the sons and daughters of this town, and the generations that are to come, tenderly bear in mind those noble men, to commemorate whose deeds this monument is erected; and as they recall to mind in future years the pioneers and builders of this place, and the sturdy families who have lived here, let them remember that upon a stable foundation only can anything valuable and beautiful securely rest.

Without a solid foundation, there can be no achievement. Without the character and strength of our ancestors, there could be no success and no beauty in our lives.

Let those who are to come after us emulate the bravery of these soldiers of the republic. Let them never forget their heroism, their patriotism, and their sacrifices. Let them grow up patriotic citizens, ever ready to respond to the demands of their town, their state, and their country, and then may the prophetic words of the great Lincoln at Gettysburg come to pass: "This nation, under God, shall have a new birth in freedom, and this government of the people, by the people, for the people, shall not perish from the earth."

Dr. Welch, in accepting the monument for the town, said,—

Honored Sir: It is with mingled emotions of joy and sorrow that I accept in behalf of your native town this noble gift, and I thank you for it:— joy, that the good old town of Sutton should have been the birthplace of one who in the broad arena of business life has courted the fickle goddess Fortune with such success as to enable him to be the donor of so noble a gift; joy, that in the full flush of honorable success his heart should turn, as fondly as does the tired infant to its mother's arms, back to his childhood's home, where rest the remains of his honored kindred;—sorrow, that the dark cloud of rebellion, which made this monument possible, should ever have swept over our fair land; sorrow, that the light of so many homes went out in darkness; sorrow, that the memory of the loved and lost is all that is left for us to-day.

It can be truly said of these men, as the poet has said of those of olden time,—

> "They left the plowshare in the mold,
> Their flocks and herds without a fold,
> Their sickles in the unshorn grain,
> Their corn half garnered on the plain,
> To right those wrongs, come weal, come woe;
> To perish, or o'ercome the foe."

The brave defenders of our liberties sleep upon every hill-top and in every valley throughout our land. Their bones lie bleaching on the frozen shores of Alaska. The tall pines of Georgia moan a midnight requiem above their lonely graves. They rest by the rocky shores of the wild Atlantic, and the mild Pacific sings its soft lullaby to their sleeping dust, while old New England holds within her rocky bosom their sacred forms.

Go where you will, from sea to sea, but tread lightly lest your foot disturb the dust of some slumbering patriot.

Have these men, who thus periled all and thus fell in the very flower of life, no claim upon the grateful remembrance of future generations? As well might we ask if the mother has any claim upon the affections of her child.

So long as human liberty is dear to the heart or education shall enlighten the mind of man, so long as freedom of opinion shall be tolerated in our land, so long as oppression shall hold the quivering heart of man in iron grasp, so long will the history of their deeds be sung in song and recounted in story. They need no monumental pile to perpetuate their memory. It is engraven upon the hearts of a grateful nation. Every school-house and college in our land; every church spire pointing heavenward; every philanthropic enterprise that we can boast; every cultivated mind that has drawn inspiration from our seats of learning; every hearth-stone throughout our broad domain, around whose cheerful light the fond mother sings the lullaby to her sleeping infant in peaceful security,—is a living, breathing monument to their patriotic devotion, that will endure as long as human hearts throb in sympathy with human woe.

Again, sir, we thank you for your noble, generous, and patriotic gift. We thank you in the name of every patriot's grave throughout our land. We thank you in the name of every battle-scarred veteran whose blood has moistened the sands of the South. We thank you in the name of every desolate fireside whose light went out in the days of the dark and bloody Rebellion. We thank you in the name of the widow and the fatherless. We thank you in the name of liberty-loving hearts throughout the world. We thank you in the name of the dear old flag, whose every star and stripe has been baptized in the blood of her patriot sons. And, sir,

> ". . . when thy summons comes to join
> The innumerable caravan that moves
> To that mysterious realm, where each shall take
> His chamber in the silent halls of death."

with a consciousness of duty well performed may you

> ". . . go not, like the quarry-slave at night,
> Scourged to his dungeon, but. . . . .
> Like one who wraps the drapery of his couch
> About him, and lies down to pleasant dreams."

Department Commander, we now turn this monument over to you for dedication to the memory of your fallen comrades. And, while the beautiful ceremony of your ritual is being enacted,

> "Memory, ever faithful to her trust,
> Will call them in beauty from the dust."

Take it, sir, and dedicate it to the memory of the loved and lost; dedicate it to the dear old flag for which they fought, and to those eternal principles of human liberty for which they fell.

The dedication of the monument followed, the beautiful and impressive ceremony being performed by Department Commander Everett B. Huse, Acting Senior Vice-Commander Frank G. Noyes, Junior Vice-Commander A. J. Sanborn, Acting Chaplain A. C. Hardy, and Assistant Adjutant-General James Minot, of the Department of New Hampshire Grand Army of the Republic.

At the conclusion of the dedication, General John Eaton was introduced as the orator of the day.

MR. EATON'S ADDRESS.

Our hearts respond to the call of this day's duty. We all come to bear a part. Our national Union, freighted with the destinies of uncounted millions of souls, was imperilled, and if it should perish the example it offered to the peoples of the earth would terminate in ruin and shame. The nation's call for defenders rang out through the land, and the sons of Sutton, with hundreds of thousands of others, rallied to the rescue, that no star should wander from the galaxy of states, nor the most promising experiment of free local self-government and representative national self-government fail among men.

Have any here to-day who either shared or witnessed, forgotten the sadness and the pain, the struggle that the last look or word might be one of cheer, as those dearest went out from their cherished homes? What future can efface the memory of that first bugle call or drum-beat, or the tramp, tramp, or their echo, lost in the shout that came up from the faithful when calls for troops were repeated,

"We are coming, Father Abraham, three hundred thousand more!"

The stars had looked on great armies marshalled as mercenaries, or as enthusiasts for conquest, by an Alexander or a Napoleon, but never on two millions of citizens,—patriots transformed to soldiers,—rushing to the defence of their free institutions. For the veterans who survive, no language of mine could add to the thrilling memories of march, camp, bivouac, hospital, siege, battle, or prison; and all the camp-fires of old soldiers will never suffice to convey to those who remained at home any adequate idea of the soldiers' experiences: they bore that other most difficult part, of toiling and of waiting.

Patriotic women could tell tales of woe to make the heart ache,—of loneliness that would not away, of cares and burthens too heavy to be borne, of the waiting for news, the anxiety over battles, and the agony when the final word left no doubt that their dearest had died in hospital, or had fallen on the field. To get any measure of the weight with which the war rested on Sutton, we need to recall that, aside from the tax paid to the state and nation, it cost the town treasury some $40,000; and that, out of a population of 1,431, one hundred and sixty-four able-bodied men went to the army,—not to count those who, natives here but resident elsewhere, joined them in rallying to the flag of the free.

Who can doubt the favor of an overruling Providence, that considers the questions which confound statesmen, or that weighs the effect of the withdrawal of so many busy hands from the farm and shop and yet sees products made abundant for home and field by improvements and methods, or marks how the national treasury was replenished and credit maintained, and sees the Union hosts finally victorious and the two contending armies dissolving and returning to the pursuits of peace, rebels forgiven, the blot of slavery forever removed from our escutcheon and the slave a citizen, the debt honestly paid, the disabled or dependent Union soldiers and their widows pensioned, and all the land rejoicing in the fruit of free institutions, the rewards of industry, and the prosperity of enterprise!

In memory of those who fell, this monument is dedicated by their surviving comrades. Quarried from the soil which they defended, these stones are reared in this graceful column to last while granite endures, the topmost chiselled into the form and position of one of their number at parade rest — never to be off duty, ready to catch, in the first rays from the king of day that wake the hopes of the morning, or in the twinkle of the most distant star of night, or in the gentle breeze of summer, or in the most heavily snow-laden blast of winter, the slightest token of evil to free institutions for which it shall stand before coming generations — an illustration of that eternal vigilance which has ever been the price of liberty.

Standing here at the dividing of the ways, it would leave no doubt, in the mind of the passer-by, which road to choose as leading to the preservation or destruction of the glorious inheritance, for the defence and transmission of which the patriots whose death it commemorates died. The population of Sutton having fallen from its largest total, or 1,573 reached in 1820 down to 993 in 1880, nearly to the 878 which it was in 1800, eighty years earlier, — the erection of a memorial so costly could hardly be expected here at public expense. But Providence, by whose favor come our liberties and their defenders, has not been unmindful of adequate and happy provision.

In observing the judicious maxim that does not permit us to pronounce final judgment upon the lives of men until they are dead, we must not be led into the error of saying no good of the living. If those who know best do not speak the truth of friends, who shall know their merits? We are a family of towns-folk here to-day, and must not consent to mar our festivities by omission. Born near this spot, taught in yonder school, reared to the severe toil which wrung an honest living from this rocky soil, accustomed to pursue with even tenor the daily tasks whether fortune favor or frown, descended from a strong and brainy ancestry, directed by a religious father, never forgotten in the instruction and prevailing prayer of a pious mother, incited towards a consecrated life by the Bible preaching and worship in the village church, a genuine product of Sutton went forth, taking as his companion one of like descent, ability, and character.

Doing duty as God gave him to see it; trusted more and more with large financial responsibility by persons and organizations; merchant, banker, trustee, mayor of the capital city of his native state, and of the largest city of that of his adoption; still cherishing as dearest the scenes of his childhood,—out of the abundance he has been permitted to gain he does what could not otherwise be expected, rears this shaft, a fit tribute to the fallen, and a silent preacher of love of country to the living. In the war for the suppression of the

Rebellion sharing the sentiments and burthens of the defenders of the Union, he now appropriately and indissolubly associates the name of George Alfred Pillsbury with the honor of those who perished. Nor is this all: his bounty has, in the name of the Master, aided domestic and foreign missions, fed the hungry, clothed the naked, and comforted the sick; the home of the orphan, and the university, have received of his gains; at his cost, Warner has its library, Concord its hospital, and Minnesota its Pillsbury academy,—and this, not from his hand cold in death, but while yet in the full enjoyment of the prosperous tide of active life.

A deficiency of hearty appreciation on our part would discount our own manhood. For myself, there is an additional reason for gratitude, an early memory more vivid than any other of him,—that of his earnest face in his young manhood in the Sunday-school, as he enforced its sacred precepts.

From the earliest times, and alike in the rudest and the most cultivated conditions, mankind have sought, by erecting monuments of the most enduring materials, to perpetuate the memory of heroic deeds. In rehearsing their sufferings and triumphs, traditions become absorbing in interest; oratory gains its power and poetry its charm. Thus imagination is filled with the best ideals, the reason is swayed by the mighty consideration of life and death, the conscience aroused in defence of right, and the will enlisted in the highest efforts of exalted manhood. In justly honoring those who die for country and for truth, we furnish one of the strongest motives that can be urged upon coming generations to emulate their virtues.

When Athens was imperilled by the aggressions of Philip, and Demosthenes would arouse his countrymen to the preservation of their liberty, he found no argument more effective than to recall the lasting gratitude and glory that had been the lot of those who laid down their lives in defence of Greece at Salamis and Marathon. We may count ourselves fortunate, that in our day one has appeared with means and desire to erect this beautiful memorial, and that we, each of us, by our presence, may range ourselves with those who enter with him into the sentiments of this occasion.

The event, moreover, is timely, in that just now, whether we seek in the past sources of present personal and civic excellence, or the inspiration to future virtuous endeavor, we have the aid of a worthy daughter of Sutton, cradled amid the virtues and intelligent aspirations of its revered fathers and mothers, taught by its teachers, who has invoked the muse of history, braved the toil of gathering the scattered data, and, with a fidelity which deserves our most hearty commendation, rescued ancestral names from oblivion, and told the story of the generations before us,—their trials, triumphs, and virtues, and how they left the town and their descendants what they are. There is an educational precept of great import, which teaches us, in seeking to know of human affairs, to follow them in their growth and by comparison, or, in other words, to study antecedents step by step, together with surroundings, bringing the whole into the most definite and comprehensive review.

Are there any whose surroundings or conceit do not permit them to see how anything great or heroic can come out of a small town, of soil so rocky, so remote from the centres of fashion, which deserves this memorial, let them consider the course of events, the growth of men and women in simplicity, purity, strength, fidelity, intelligence, and piety in the tonic of these elevated valleys, rugged hills and ledgy mountains, and primeval forests, where we must confess there has too often seemed to be, in the thoughts of some, nothing in human existence but work, where the whole family has appeared to struggle for the bare necessaries of life, the father's toil bowing his stalwart frame and the mother's work never done.

I rejoice in the spirit that is waking up to the study of our local history. It will administer wholesome doses of wisdom to many a growing folly. Nothing is easier than to forget. Nothing is harder than experience, save the learning of its lessons from those who have gone before. The truth that fire burns is of little value to the child till he has put his own hand in the flame.

The sons and daughters of Sutton should be deceived by no sickly sentimentality, that can see greatness and excellence only when born with the proverbial silver spoon, or clothed in silk, or housed in palaces, or rolling in princely equipage. They should understand their birthright, and sell it not for any mess of pottage. Let them understand the rock out of which they are hewn. The results in which we find satisfaction to-day have not come by chance. As certainly as this memorial finds its sure foundation in the supporting earth beneath, so surely are there ancestral causes for the virtues which it would perpetuate. In its presence we can do no better service to honor its giver or the memory of our patriot dead, than to trace the path that leads them to excellence, and with fidelity to preserve it ourselves and lead our children therein. Take these Sutton volumes: trace their results back through the Puritan upheaval in England, the Roman conquest, and the displacement of paganism by Christianity,—and there comes in a flood of light on human experience to add wisdom to the wisest.

Sutton may be taken as an illustration of the settlement of the interior New England towns; and, if the founders of Rome were worthy to be sung by a Virgil, these early settlers deserve a poet as much greater, as their motives and ends were more exalted,—as much as the American nation excels in beneficence the power that ruled the world from the seven hills on the banks of the Tiber. Analyze the early settler of Sutton, and you will find in him all the elements of the Englishman of the seventeenth century, increased by a hundred and fifty years of colonial experience on these rock-bound shores under the influence of that compact signed by the Pilgrims on the Mayflower, in which all citizens were to take equal part in a government that should derive its powers from the governed,—thus dispensing with the trumpery of thrones and the oppressions of classes, substituting the divinity of personal rights for the divine right of kings.

In the veins of the Sutton settler as he first crossed the spur of Kearsarge from the earlier settlements along the Merrimack, or later as he came by Warner, you would find coursing the blood to which the original Breton, Saxon, Dane, and Norman had contributed. He took up land as left by the savage, and at first lived, much like him, upon game and the rude products of nature: forests went down, cabins went up. His superiority appeared, as his social, civil, and religious life developed. The church and school sprang up side by side, the family was sacred, the road connected home with home and with all the world beside; every man participated in local self-government, while by the representative elected by the majority he shared in the action of the general court that provided laws for all the towns.

One philosopher informs us, with emphasis, that "The first farmer was the first man, and all historic nobility rests on possession and use of land." Another affirms, of primitive peoples, "Those are slower in attaining civilization to whom nature has denied domestic animals, flocks, and herds of cattle." These cond'tions our fathers enjoyed to the utmost. Study the contents of their minds in the outcome of their theories, industries, customs, and institutions, and there will be found traces of contribution from the code of Moses and the precepts of Christianity, the Roman jus civile, the Saxon tithing, hundred and court, the charter of rights wrung by the barons from King John, and the triumph of the ironsides and statesmanship of Cromwell. If we read "Paradise Lost" with the recollection that it was written by the blind bard under the shadow of the restoration of corrupt monarchy, we shall gain a deeper impression of the significance of the reaction from the Puritan uplift. A historian most hostile to Christianity frankly confesses, "The precious spark of liberty had been kindled and was preserved by the Puritans alone, and that it was to this sect that the English owe the freedom of their constitution.

'Even the peasant came his rights to scan,
And learned to enumerate himself a man.'"

They held every man accountable before God, whether peasant or king. Vice and crime, as they saw them, were everywhere to be smitten by divine wrath. At that date no race could excel the English speaking people in gathering the fruit of human progress. As the ocean swept all sides of their island home, so the tides in men's affairs had brought them the best results in brawn and brain, and in personal rights, both civil and religious. None had a freer person or conscience, none could use better freedom of opinion or speech. Early in possession of the art of printing and of a translation of the Scriptures into his native tongue, he employed the one to disseminate the other, that all might read who run.

All schemes of colonization fell behind the English, and none approached in far-reaching result, those of New England. Says a recent European writer, "It was characteristic, that the really organizing forces were generated in New England;— under sterner, barer, and altogether harder conditions, they developed much the earlier into settled communities, loving order, culture, and all the fairer amenities of life. Throughout, they remained less mercantile and more intellectual; their love of education amounted to a passion." Massachusetts, as a leading colony, whether in harmony or antagonism in its relations to the crown, gained wisdom from every turn of affairs in England or on the Continent. The New Hampshire Plantations for a time shared in the legislation of the Massachusetts general court, and when under an administration of their own, moved along the same line of policy.

The common law of England went with every English speaking colonist. The error of persecuting Baptists and Quakers and of burning witches had disappeared before the Sutton fathers had entered upon their task. Only eight years had elapsed after the first settlement, when the Battle of Bunker Hill called them to arms against the mother country in defence of their dearly bought rights. But, made of the stuff they were, wrought into the characters as we have so briefly noted, we are ready to believe, few and exposed as they were to savage enemies, that they were prepared fearlessly to bear their part wherever the fortunes of war for the dedefence of their liberties might call them. Well might the orator exclaim, "The cause will raise up armies, the cause will equip navies." Well might the Earl of Chatham in the midst of his eloquent periods startle his associates with the declaration, "You cannot conquer America."

The patriots had not passed through the fiery furnace of oppression in vain. Burke, remarking on the growth of political thought in America, called attention to the large sale of copies of Blackstone law commentaries in the colonies. In an important sense, the men who have gone before us, whether their lives have ended in peace or in war, are not dead.

> "Cold in the dust the perished heart may lie.
> But that which warmed it once can never die."

The men of peace are necessary to those of war: each prepares for the other. The maxim to which Washington lent the weight of his wisdom—" In peace prepare for war "—has its counterpart in the declaration that a just war, one in defence of human rights, is a preparation for peace. The years from the War of Independence to 1860 may be said to have been one long period of preparation for the death struggle for the Union.

The war had its demoralizing effect; its obligations to creditors and to its long-suffering patriotic soldiers were unpaid; families were broken up, and reduced to poverty and suffering by the loss of their male support; industries, trade, schools, and churches were interrupted;—but the forward step taken for mankind was enormous. Its significance grew upon the public mind. By degrees, religious, moral, and patriotic sentiment began to awaken, and take into account the new aspect of affairs. The Confederate congress, under which the colonies, transformed into states, had carried on the war and won independence, unable to levy taxes or enforce its own laws, had sufficed to show that it was powerless to preserve a national existence against internal dissension, and admonished statesmen and people of its need of revision. However feeble its power, the great spirits in it were equal to the occasion.

By the skilful diplomacy of the American commissioners, in the negotiations of the treaty of peace with Great Britain, that vast territory northwest of the Ohio river, known in England as "The back lands of Canada," out of which six of our great states have been formed, had been secured to the United States against the original desire of Spain, France, and England. In the darkest days of the war, Washington said among his soldiers, "If British oppression drives us from our homes on the Atlantic sea-board, we will retire beyond the mountains and the Ohio, and set up there a government of free men." A number of his soldiers formed the Ohio company, and sought to purchase there, and settle, a million and a half of acres, paying chiefly in the paper obligations issued for military services. Washington approved the project. The Continental congress made the sale, and, in providing a government, passed the great act distinguished in history as the Ordinance of 1787. It gathered up and applied to this vast region, an empire in itself, the best provisions found in the enactments of all the colonies.

The law of primogeniture, which limited inheritance to the oldest son, was abolished, and intestate estates were to descend in equal parts to all the children, male and female alike, thus restoring a privilege to woman not recognized since the laws of Moses. No property was to be taken for public use save by due process of law and on just compensation; severe punishment was forbidden; national right to navigable waters was enforced; Indians were to be treated with fairness; morality and religion were to be encouraged; schools and universities were to be established, and sections of land appropriated for their support; and slavery was forever forbidden. Our national history has turned on this enactment as on a hinge. Its educational policy has been applied to all the states since formed. It has reacted on all the older states, to bring their laws up to its standard.

Its provisions, as they became known, were heartily approved by the people, and exerted a powerful influence in shaping the constitution, for whose formation in convention and adoption by the states, as well as the election of a president and congress under it, these noble patriots provided in laying off the authority with which they had been clothed. Every hamlet in the wide land felt the effect of these significant events. Credit was restored, industry was rewarded, enterprises multiplied. New fields invited the pioneer. As the years passed, additional territory was acquired. Foreign powers felt the growth of a new free government in America. Monarchs and aristocrats might prophesy its early ruin, but its growth in mighty proportions went on. Millions caught new hope from its rising stars, and founded happy families under its protection. The critic might sneeringly ask, "Who reads an American book?" or the traveller might sting with criticism the hand that had welcomed him.

Hospitality did not abate, culture increased, science advanced, books and authors multiplied. The New England passion for education went West with the men and women that founded new states. It has been stated that there are communities where education is universal and compulsory, in which the intelligence thus gained is so little brought into use in after-life that much of it is lost and the ability to read and write disappears. When Charles the Bold was killed and his army defeated, it is related that the soldier who captured the royal diamond, then of almost unexampled size, was so unaware of its value that he sold it for a florin. Not so in America: the intelligent soldier knew for what he fought, and what he gained. The citizen has too many demands upon his information not to increase year by year what the school has taught him.

National parties formed and re-formed; personal ambitions and local animosities appeared and disappeared. There were discussions in the press, among the people, and between the giants in congress over various issues, but behind all there could be discovered a growing difference, greater and more fundamental than all others, and affecting all—irreconcilable and irrepressible. The formation of opinion along the solid line which accepted the doctrine that a divine sacrifice was equally necessary for every soul, thus confirming the belief in the brotherhood of man, had led to the abolition of slavery in the Eastern and Middle states, and the Ordinance of 1787 forbade its admission into the territory controlled by it, while the constitution prohibited the slave trade on the high seas, protected slavery where it existed, and left its regulation to the states. The South found it increasingly profitable, as improvements in machinery gave new value to the culture of cotton. Thus two great civilizations had grown up, and now hastened toward the final struggle for supremacy. Great patriots foresaw the threatened appeal to arms, and sought to avert the outbreak by delay.

But with the tide of civilization rising and these differences becoming more pronounced, we must not forget to ask, What of Sutton during these nearly fourscore years, as the character of the citizen-soldier, as represented in this memorial, approaches completion? During this period our Sutton fathers were so prepared to be a self-supporting, self-contained community, that, in addition to the duties of the family and the farm, to which the women and the men were mainly devoted, over thirty other occupations have been counted among them. Could we pause to enumerate, there would be "the surgeon of old shoes" and the maker of new ones; the mason, whose "bricks are alive at this day to testify;" the tailor, who "makes all we see of many men;" the teacher, whose familiarity with the oil of birch is too great to need the exhortation of the poet,—

> "O ye who teach the ingenuous youth of nations,
> I pray ye flog them on occasions;
> It mends their morals—never mind the pain."

And here, too, is the grave-digger—

"The houses he makes last till doomsday."

Here, too, also, the joiner and carpenter: would not he smile at the mention that "chest or house is better finished than his"? And here, too, is the smith, to make

"The spade, the ploughshare, and the rake."

Nor is the physician or preacher wanting, nor, for once, the printer and almanac maker. Bargains might be sharp, but honesty was the best policy. The cheat was unpardoned: the town early procured standards of weights and measures. The idler was abhorred: children at their mother's breast imbibed the safe doctrine that Satan employed the idle. The sentiment was universal, that there is not to be an honest living without labor. They made it their task "To see the sun to bed and to rise." It was

"Work, work, work,
While the cock is crowing aloof;
And work, work, work
Till the stars shine through the roof."

save when the Sabbath brought the needed pause, and the whole family, on foot or on horse-back, or, later, in wagon or chaise, wended their way to meeting. The youth may sometimes have feared that their elders had adopted only a part of those noted lines.

"All play and no work makes Jack a mere toy;
All work and no play makes Jack a dull boy."

But strength and health of body and mind, honest toil, a clear conscience, assured supply of daily wants though simple, the consolation of a Bible faith, were not without solid enjoyment and good cheer, which many a man cannot find amid the greatest luxuries that wealth can buy. It is not in poetry alone that we learn how

"The jocund swain drives his team afield."

But Sutton folks were not without occasions when they let nature caper. Even these might smack of the busy bee, for were there not the apple-bee, husking-bee, and bees without name, not to mention the sewing-circle, spelling-school, singing-school, Fourth of July, May training and regimental muster, town-meeting, and Thanksgiving Day? Uncle Sam, who receives and delivers his mail in the remotest corner of his vast domain,— though it came not here daily, or perhaps weekly, and then not in an express train thundering through the valleys and hills,—early began to bring the letter of business and friendship and the weekly gazette, even when he could only afford a carrier on horseback, who announced his approach by the blast from his horn. Before this century began, a social library was established, and its books, though not numerous, were of standard merit. There are those now alive who have walked twelve miles to borrow from its shelves.

These books, added to the Bible,—not then the hiding-place for lost spectacles,—added to Watts, Bunyan, Doddridge or Edwards, Paley or Clark, Addison or Shakespeare, left the reading homes

not without nourishing intellectual food, while the
newspaper kept them abreast with the progress of
the world at large. Not a few committed to memory large portions of Scripture and of standard
authors. I have heard a sainted grandmother, on
her death-bed, repeat before prayer the lengthy
chapter she desired. I have heard a most unpretending man repeat page after page from the standard poets. How many gems of literature were gathered from familiar school-readers! Only recently, a
man advanced beyond middle life, visiting the town
with his wife, younger in years, greeting an unassuming farmer friend by the way, was surprised
beyond his own knowledge by an apt quotation
from Parnell, an old poet little known:

> "While in their age they differ, join in heart;
> Thus stands an aged elm in ivy bound,
> Thus useful vigor clasps the elm around."

Sutton youth have not been without the highest
aspirations for culture. The first generation of
children was represented in Dartmouth college.
In the town-meeting, that school for patriots, they
voted for president or for representative in congress,
state and county officers, and elected of their own
number for the service of the town. They built
and repaired their own roads, conducted their own
schools, laid their own taxes, and, when they chose,
passed resolutions upon the questions of state and
national policy, such as temperance and anti-slavery. They were men of deeds, not words; but gain
a knowledge of their thoughts, and you would find
among them carefully matured opinions on the

questions of their times as well as on the fundamental doctrines of life. They were alert for debate in the political campaign, and had a hearty appreciation of the ablest speakers.

The Athenians might depend upon the market-place, and the Romans add, for their gossip, the opportunities furnished for conversation in their luxurious baths, some of whose massive ruins still remain. Our fathers emphasized the value of time: its loss was perilous, and it could not be recovered, and without idling they enjoyed the exchange of neighborhood news in the social moments about their meetings, at the store, the mill, or the smithy. No child could grow up in neglect. Was parental control for any reason wanting, the officer took the child in charge, and placed him in a worthy family to work, to attend the district school, and to be trained in the way he should go. Vice or crime was little known. There was great pride of self-support, but the needy were not allowed to suffer. Thus were formed the men whose patriotic death we honor. Every generation made its contribution of men and women to every vocation, in all parts of the land, and to honorable public service. Of the first generation of children, one son of Matthew Harvey presided over the senate, while the other presided over the house of representatives, of their state; both became members of congress; one was a governor, and was also United States district judge for over a generation.

Would you understand what these backwoods New Hampshire towns have contributed to the uplift of mankind, place yourself on the summit of

Kearsarge yonder, and count the men and women of mark who have been born or lived within fifty miles, and try, if you can, anywhere else, among the same number of people, in the same area, to find a similar result. Here is a president and a chief-justice of the United States, and members of the cabinet; here are governors and members of congress, judges, teachers, inventors, financiers, leaders on the farm and in the shop, and in every other honorable pursuit in life; while above all others towers Daniel Webster, God-like in intellect, whose profound and patriotic interpretations of the constitution furnished the arguments on which rested the sentiment of the statesmen and soldiers who saved the Union.

As this noble gift, bestowed by a native of Sutton resident in a distant state, is received with heartiest thanks by those who remain to keep up the old landmarks, and all those scattered abroad meet with those at home in most hearty greeting, are we not admonished that both, in a sense, have the dear old town in their keeping? There may be a welcome for those who return, that will increase their coming and doing. It has been characteristic of men in all ages, as they approach the grave, to desire to return to the scenes their childhood held dear. They walk by the old wandering fences, hunt the deserted paths, and fondly muse among the objects that recall scenes and friends of other days.

Dr. Horace Eaton said,—"Wandering in a neglected field, I came to a forsaken cellar. There were sermons in those stones. They were carefully laid by my own father's hands. Here he erected his humble dwelling, in which my parents began their married life. Here six of my older brothers and sisters were born. Here occurred the first death in our family. How much of history is unwritten! What labors, joys, sorrows, sympathies, charities, could be evoked from that old cellar! Here, was a cheerful hearth-stone. Here, the Bible, the hymn-book, the catechism, and prayer had their place. On the grassy lawn the children used to sport. Near by, a rosebush showed where once the garden smiled. Five of us brothers and sisters once gathered here, and marked where our mother used to plant the coarse and honest sunflower, the erect and soldier-like hollyhock, the flaming poppy, the curt pink, and the gorgeous peony. But now, save the rose and the lilac and tansy, the nettle, the mullein, and the elecampane possess this sacred soil. Farewell to this old and lonely cellar!"

Said Daniel Webster, referring to the home of his birth,—" Its remains still exist. I make to it an annual visit. I carry my children to it, to teach them the hardships endured by the generations which have gone before them. I love to dwell on the tender recollections, the kindred ties, the early affections, and the touching narratives and incidents which mingle with all I know of this primitive family abode. I weep to think that none of those who inhabited it are among the living."

May there not be hope for these deserted but sacred places, in the restful summer return and reunion of the absent sons and daughters? The soil has already proved its endurance: no state has reported a larger product of corn to an acre. With appropriate diversity of skilful industry, farming, and raising men and women, must remain the chief business for Sutton. If the fathers had the skill to coin money out of the forest,—turning trees into ashes, and these into lye, and that into potash,—shall not their sons more readily turn into coin their beautiful scenery, pure water, healthful tonic climate, by multiplying the attractions to summer residents?

We are forced to recognize the fact that the sleepers in the Sutton villages of the dead outnumber the living. On the great truth that "One generation grows while one decays," rests our hope of human affairs. Every token of excellence attained increases the means of making what is to be more honorable than what has been. One people above all others stands before the world as an illustration of the preservation of the identity of race characteristics. Whatever the laws of heredity may have accomplished for them is increased by the faithful communication of instruction and training from father to son. For ages, when the child has asked what may be the meaning of this or that memorial, the parent has rehearsed its story and repeated it line upon line. Thus, as years pass, when the child shall ask, What means this soldiers' monument? let the story be rehearsed. Give him all he can know of the deeds of valor of those in the field and the fidelity of those in the home, and of the generosity of its giver. Let him see how "a thousand years scarce serves to form a state" that "an hour may lay in the dust."

The story of Washington and his associates, their examples of heroism and statesmanship, added to the glow with which the past filled the memory and imagination of the fathers. Thus shall the late war, its Lincoln and Grant and their associates, their statesmanship and deeds of valor, increase patriotic ardor and sacrifice, as their memory goes down in tradition, in song, and in history to the latest times. Thus shall all the monuments reared to Union soldiers unite with this in proclaiming the righteousness of their cause and the value of the liberties they preserved,—nay, and the memorials reared by admiring friends to the disloyal, telling of their valor but preserving the memory of their error,—and shall add their testimony to the stupendous magnitude of the contest in which they engaged, and most solemnly warn against any steps leading to its repetition.

So shall it be true as commanded:

Remember the days of old; consider the years of many generations; ask thy father, and he shall show thee thy elders, and they will tell thee.

Thus may it be, that this memorial to the memory of the deeds we this day honor shall aid in perpetuating our institutions of liberty, as the protection and hope of the free and the brave, to that day when human government shall be no more, wherein the heavens shall be dissolved and the elements melt with fervent heat.

The following poem, written for the occasion by Mrs. Augusta Harvey Worthen, author of the History of Sutton, was read by her nephew, Charles H. Kohlrausch, Jr., of Billerica, Mass.:

1861 AND 1891.

A sound of fierce conflict the nation alarms:
Our country is calling. "To Arms! Fly to Arms!"
In deadliest peril her cry ringeth forth,—
Oh! haste to her rescue, ye men of the North!

From the hills of the Northland the men hurry down,
From each quiet hamlet and each busy town;
Unmindful of self, never waiting to grieve
For the sorrowing friends and the dear homes they leave.

Went two and thirty Sutton men, but ere the war was o'er,
The number of their names had reached one hundred
    sixty-four;
Though some men had been wounded sore, and some (more
    blest) were killed.
Each call for help was promptly met, and every quota filled.

For even in that darkest year, when hope had almost fled,
And when from many a Northern home rose wailings for
    their dead.
When abroad o'er the land came again and again
The president's call,—"More men—more men!"

Not once old Sutton the claim denies,—
She yields up the costly sacrifice.
Their doom of death or suffering not given her to know,
Her mother-heart is breaking, but she bids her children go.

And so her sons, still undismayed, joined, as they marched
    along,
With North, and East, and West, to sing that grand, soul-
    stirring song.—

That song whose glorious echoes rolled from mountain top
 to shore,—
"We are coming, Father Abraham, three hundred thousand
 more!"

We know the story of the war—how its varying fortunes
 turned;
We feel the debt of gratitude our soldiers richly earned.
Shall their valiant deeds forgotten be, 'mong the homes
 they helped to save?
Can we give them nothing nobler than a pension and
 a grave?

Nigh thirty years has Sutton stood, since the closing of the
 war,—
Stood looking from her lofty hills, to see in towns afar
The sculptured monuments appear, such as only wealth
 can raise,
To stand throughout all coming time, and speak their
 soldiers' praise.

And then, like any mother's, has her heart within her
 burned:
"Why see I not my sons receive the glory that they earned?
Their deeds as grand and noble were, their sacrifice as
 great,—
To see their merits recognized, how long, how long I wait!"

But one there was who, in his home 'neath a far off Western sky,
O'er the miles of half a continent, could hear that mother-
 cry;
He heard that cry and felt that call, and then his purpose
 grew,
For Sutton's sons his brethren were, and she his mother, too.

He "looked, and saw not one to help;" then said he, "Lo!
 I come!
Myself a monument will build, close by my native home,

For all our Sutton soldiers, where'er they fought or bled,
Wherever they be living, wherever they be dead."

To-day he gives us this great gift; we take the sacred trust:
We'll guard it with the reverent care we give our soldiers'
　　dust.
So long, so long through the coming years,
As this granite base its shaft uprears,
This spot shall consecrated be
To our Sutton soldiers' memory;
And this the rallying-place shall be
For all the "Sons of Liberty."

Hither on each Memorial Day
Shall the Grand Army comrades wend their way,
And here our nation's flag display;
Shall list to strains of eloquence,
And, if our country needs defence,
Shall here to loyal zeal be fired
And here to patriot deeds inspired.

Now Sutton is turning her motherly face
　　From the beautiful gift to the giver;
And this is the message she charges me
　　(Her handmaid) to deliver.

My son, no words can speak the pride,
　　The joy I have in thee,
As well for the good done far and wide
　　As the good thou hast done for me.

I have watched thy course these many days,
　　I know thou hast done well;
For I have listened and caught every word of praise
　　That from grateful lips has fell.

Thou hast fed the hungry, and clothed the poor,
　　And for feeble childhood cared;
And more feeble old age has thy bounteous store
　　And thy thoughtful kindness shared.

Forerunning the time when all pain shall cease.
    Thou hast hospitals built and given,
Where the homeless sick find rest and peace
    That seems like the peace of heaven.

The blessing of him that was ready to perish
    Hath oft and again come to thee ;
Thou religion and learning dost foster and cherish,
    That the world may the better be.

The wealth and the power at thy command
    Thou but holdest, as if in trust,
For the cause, remote or near at hand,
    That merits or needs it most.

Often as came the call for help,
    Thy deed hath made reply,—
"Is any wanting to thy work ?
    Take me, Lord: here am I."

Like Joseph, rich with favors rare
    From Pharaoh, Egypt's king,
Thou too wouldst have the brethren share
    The honors thou canst bring.

For this, my son, my thanks receive,
For this I now my blessing give :
Through life the favor of our Lord
Be thine exceeding great reward.

Hon. Nehemiah George Ordway, a native of Warner, who from 1880 till 1884 served as governor of what is now the two states of North and South Dakota, and who, in his executive journeyings between the two capitals of Yankton and Bismarck, made frequent neighborly visits to his old friends and townsmen, Gov. John S. Pillsbury and Mayor George A. Pillsbury, of Minneapolis, was called upon by the president, and spoke substantially as follows:

Mr. President, and Old Friends around the base and sides of grand old Kearsarge Mountain: I shall not allow myself to make a speech, fearing that it might mar the exhaustive oration you have just listened to from my old school-mate, General John Eaton.

I should, however, do violence to my feelings if I should fail to respond to your kind but unexpected invitation to say a few words expressive of the great satisfaction with which I have listened to these beautiful dedicatory exercises, and feasted my eyes upon this symmetrical monument.

It has been my privilege to hold friendly relations for more than forty years with this Pillsbury family, both in this our native county, and in the new homes we have made among the golden wheat-fields of the new North-west. I have congratulated Governor John S., and rejoiced with the ex-mayor of Concord, George Alfred, when elected mayor of the new Western metropolis, Minneapolis, and I extend to both here to-day, and to their good wives, to whom they and I are so largely indebted, the warmest congratulations upon this auspicious occasion.

As I gaze with admiration upon this beautiful soldiers' monument, encircled by the veterans of the Union army, and located just in front of the old church on the common of this cosy hamlet, surrounded by these everlasting hills, and realize that these solemn Grand Army exercises will go down the vista of time with the name of George Alfred

Pillsbury, the generous donor, I feel that Warner, where he made his first home, has a strong interest in him, and a right to rejoice with Sutton, his birthplace, at the continued success of such a son, who has returned to the old homestead and erected this monument, and now places it with a loving hand as a gift to the place of his nativity.

It is an undisputed fact, which has gone into history, that the birth-places of more men and women who have made themselves names and become distinguished can be seen and recognized from the clean granite summit of yonder Kearsarge mountain, at a point where four large towns are bounded, than from any other spot in the world; and the additional fact is demonstrated here to-day, by those who are here to honor this occasion, that the stock is not deteriorating.

I am advised that the artisan who drew the plan, by the aid of Mr. Pillsbury, and fashioned these beautiful blocks with a soldier surmounting the top, as a lesson to those who are to come after us, was a Sutton boy also, and that he is here to-day to witness these memorable exercises, and to receive the commendations upon his work from his former neighbors and friends.

Mr. President, realizing that my personal friend and official neighbor in the West, who filled the executive chair in the thriving state of Minnesota by three consecutive elections for six years, and whose name is written upon so many pages of the records of that great state, Gov. John S. Pillsbury, is here to honor this occasion, and will speak to you as old neighbors and friends, I will close by congratulating the people of this good old town upon the success of these Memorial Exercises and upon their generous hospitality.

Hon. John S. Pillsbury, of Minneapolis, Minn., was introduced, and spoke as follows:

MR. CHAIRMAN, SOLDIERS OF THE GRAND ARMY, LADIES AND GENTLEMEN: It is forty-eight years since I left this my native village. It was in the little red school-house, just yonder (it was red then), that I attended school, and there it was that I acquired my education. Then, our happy family were all living. To-day, my brother and I are all that are left. The rest sleep in yonder cemetery. There are, indeed, many pleasant recollections, and there are also many, very many, sad ones, which come to us to-day. The monument which we here dedicate will perpetuate the memory of many of those whom you still mourn, and it will remind our youth of the valiant deeds done on the battle-field by the hardy yeomen of New England for the preservation of the Union. I did not have the honor to serve my country under arms as you served it, but I did the most that I could to aid and support those who did, and I am proud to belong to an organization similar to yours.

The defenders of our country have rendered most gallant services, not only on the battle-field, but also in the legislative deliberations of our nation. To those hard-working, methodical husbandmen of New England who fought seven years for independence, we are indebted for the passage of the Ordinance of 1787, referred to by the orator of the day. The immortal Jefferson, in 1784, first drafted an ordinance for the admission of the North-western Territory. He provided in it, that after the year 1800 neither slavery nor involuntary servitude should be allowed within the limits of that broad domain. This ordinance was introduced into congress in 1784, and was defeated in that year and in the subsequent year by the votes of the Southern states, on account of its prohibition of slavery. In 1787 the old soldiers of New England resolved to carry the measure through, and when led by such men as Putnam, Cutler, and their associates, with the support of Washington, they made known their wants to congress. The soldiers of the South rallied to the support of their old comrades in arms, and passed the measure. Think, now, how far reaching were the provisions of that ordinance. Among them were these: That land should be set aside for the maintenance of the public schools in every township, for religious purposes, and for a university, and that slavery should be forever prohibited within the limits of the new territory. Who shall estimate the services rendered by these heroes of the Revolutionary War in securing the passage of this ordinance! In that vast region six great commonwealths,—Ohio, Michigan, Indiana, Illinois, Wisconsin, and Minnesota,—were soon reared—over the latter of which, Minnesota, I have had the honor to preside—and when the cruel war came they were all loyal to the Union. Without their aid the Union could not have been preserved, for it was slavery that caused the war.

It is now more than twenty-five years since the close of that terrible civil war. I often wonder how many of the millions of the young men at this day appreciate the perils of that struggle, and realize at what a cost of life and treasure the Union was preserved; how many have read the history of that war and of this country. I would make it obligatory that every district school in this broad land should teach the history of our country as the first study. For three hundred years the schools of Greece taught their children the story of Leonidas and his followers, who sacrificed their lives at Thermopylae. Is it of less importance that our children should be taught lessons of valor and of patriotism from the battles of our struggles for Independence, the War of 1812, and the Civil War? From these, and from the innumerable resting-places of the valiant dead to whose heroic deeds inscribed shafts of marble are raised, our youth should learn at what a terrible sacrifice of life and treasure this Union was established and has been preserved.

We hear agitation for the division of the public-school fund in the West. It is advocated by certain religious orders. You have the same agitation here in the East. This must not be. Who has travelled abroad and not noticed the absence of the school-house! In Ireland there are but few; in Scotland, England, Belgium, and France, but few more. In Italy there are none at all. There the state and the hierarchy largely do the thinking for the people. Parochial schools are the medium of education. But in America, the land of the free, we teach man to think for himself. Our government is of the people, by the people, and for the people—a land of peace and plenty, where the public schools are always open free to the youth. Our public schools are the sheet anchor of our national liberty, and that liberty can only be preserved by keeping the fund by which they are maintained intact, as it now is. Let our watchword be, No division of the public-school funds; millions for the public schools as long as they are built, as they now are, in every hamlet throughout this broad land, and remain with open doors free to all for the general education of our youth.

Mr. Chairman, I have been exceedingly pleased with the exercises of the day. It has been a day of great enjoyment to all who have been here. Especially do I desire to thank the ladies for the sumptuous repast to which we were invited in the tent, and for their attention, and for the beautiful flowers which decorated the tables. I am sure that every one in this great assembly joins with me in tendering these thanks.

I thank you, Mr. Chairman, for the courtesy of your invitation to be here and to speak.

Charles E. Cummings, the architect and builder of the monument, spoke as follows:

MR. CHAIRMAN, AND FELLOW-CITIZENS OF MY NATIVE TOWN: I have been requested to make a statement about the monument,—as to what kind of granite it is made of, where the design was procured, etc. About eighteen months ago the donor of this memorial gift wrote me that he was desirous of presenting to his native town of Sutton some token of his esteem, and suggested that perhaps a soldiers' monument would be as acceptable as anything that he might do for it. He accordingly requested me to prepare some designs, for his inspection, of different monuments erected to the memory of soldiers of the late war. I did so, and when he again visited his native state he examined them. There were five designs, and, after a careful inspection of all of them, the one finally selected is that which now stands before you. I think no mistake was made in accepting this design. Four of the designs were of monuments standing in various towns in New England, while the fifth was made in my office, and is the one represented here, and its duplicate is not standing anywhere else. This design was made by taking certain parts of different monuments and making a new one. Some of the parts were taken from the Londonderry soldiers' monument, in Rockingham county, this state, and some from monuments I saw at Quincy and Marlborough, Mass., and at Barre, Vt. The selection of the best points in these several monuments, being properly proportioned, made a new design of pleasing effect. The beauty of a monument, as of a building, is to have all its parts so constructed as to harmonize the whole work. The material may be good, the workmanship the best, but if the proportions are not correct the whole structure is a failure;—and the same may be said by reversing the statement: If proportions are good, and the material and workmanship are faulty, then the work is not a success. But if proportions, materials, and workmanship are all what they should be, then you will obtain a beautiful structure. This monument is built of Concord granite, with the exception of the die, which is made of Quincy granite. The curbing and foundation are made of your own King's Hill granite. The whole height is about thirty-two feet. The soldier is in position of "parade rest." The cannon balls, cap, and crossed sabres are emblems of war; the laurel wreaths encircling the shaft are emblems of peace after victory.

My very high regard for the giver of this memorial, and my appreciation of the services of the men of my native town who bravely fought for country and for home, were sufficient incentives for me to do the best I could in making this monument. How well I have succeeded is for others to say. It was very gratifying to me that I had an opportunity to do what little I have done in connection with this noble gift to the town in memory of her soldiers. I was well acquainted with them all when they enlisted in the great struggle that followed, and I have ever held them in grateful remembrance. Some lost their lives in the conflict, and never returned to dear friends left at home; some are honored citizens of this and other towns; many returned with impaired health; others have since crossed the last picket-line, have heard the last bugle-call, and have passed the portals of the mysterious unknown. This monument, dedicated to-day, will ever stand, a lasting memorial of their sacrifices, their courage, and their patriotism, until time shall be no more.

Colonel Frank G. Noyes, of Nashua, spoke in behalf of the Grand Army of the Republic as follows:

COMMANDER AND FRIENDS: I am aware that most of you must be weary, standing as you have for nearly three hours participating in the beautiful ceremonies of the day. Therefore I feel heavily handicapped in responding to the request of the Department Commander to speak for the Grand Army. Both duty and inclination urge me to say a few words for the old boys in blue, and the hearty reception so warmly extended by my comrades here must be my apology, if any be needed.

It often happens, my friends, that a wayfarer, following a beaten track, or threading a wilderness, comes to a milestone, or an acclivity, where, laying down his bundle, he takes a seat, wipes the sweat from his brow, and surveys the landscape. If the sun has passed the zenith, he looks back to recognize, if possible, those points in his journey marked by some exceptional effort he has made, a peril he has passed through. He looks for the frail bridges he has crossed, the fords he has waded, and the quagmires he has floundered through. He seeks the points where he and his companions, who started with him, parted company, and strives, by signs of those in sight, and by halloos to those in hearing, to bid them another God-speed. This is the journey of a day, but it is also the journey of a life.

We are here to-day, my comrades, like the wayfarer, to pause from our usual avocations, and aid in dedicating this structure, erected in memory of some of those who started with us, engaged in the same cause, shared the same dangers, bore the same hardships, but have parted company with us and answered the last roll-call.

We claim that the cause of the veteran is the cause of the country. In the days of great peril, when the hand of the traitor had its deadly grip on the throat of the nation, our government did not draw the line at any race, creed, politics, color, or cost of the volunteer. The cost was not counted; the government was prodigal of money and lavish of blood; and the man who enlisted was the hero of the hour. As was lately said in congress, "To-day there is not a loyal veteran soldier or sailor of the republic to whom the republic is not a debtor." How much more the republic is indebted to those heroes who yielded up their lives for their country, a few of whom this monument was erected to honor, and whose precious memories we are aiding to commemorate!

What memories both pleasant and sad, what loving thoughts and tender recollections, crowd upon us, both citizen and soldier, as we join in the ceremonies of this day, which dedicate, to the patriotism and valor of the men of Sutton, this tribute of respect! It is not so very long ago since they went forth in the pride and strength of their young manhood to do valiant battle for country and for right. And according to the measure of their strength, we believe that they all did their duty. Some there were, alas! who faltered and laid down their arms; but it was at the command of duty.

My friends, the life-work of the veterans of the

Union army and navy is nearly done. Sorrow and the soldier daily pass over many a threshold; and across the land are many homes made desolate. Those of us who remain are but the reserves, who, on occasions like this, in recalling a common sacrifice and final triumph, repeat that story of heroic endeavor which will rekindle the spirit of American patriotism in generations yet to come.

Comrades, in these modern days of image-breaking, history is being doubted and traditions laughed at. By the same token, our own achievements will be attacked, after the lapse of a century or two, and some of the events that we absolutely know to have occurred will be doubted. As was said by ex-Senator Palmer not long ago,—"Men are beginning to ask, Was Nero really a monster? or Richard the Lion-hearted a bad man? Benedict Arnold finds apologists, and Aaron Burr defenders. William Tell has been relegated to the realm of myths; and Mazeppa, dear to every youthful heart, is now said never to have taken the ride which he imposed as truth on Charles XII." Within a month it has been gravely stated in some of the newspapers that the name of the wife of Gen. John Stark, whose great achievement at Bennington has just been commemorated, was not "Molly" at all, and that therefore "Molly" Stark could never have slept a widow. In view of these things, there is one order that cannot be given too often to the old veterans who fought for the flag. I therefore venture to repeat it, and that command is,—" Guard well your faith; stand to your colors." Believe in yourselves, act for yourselves; and remember, as Miles Standish found out to his sorrow, that a sweetheart courted by proxy is a sweetheart lost.

The memory of those heroes who have crossed the last river and reported to the great Commander on the other side, whether they yielded up their lives in battle, in hospital, or surrounded by loving hearts and tender hands at home, is kept fresh and green by surviving comrades and faithful friends. Choice offerings are daily laid at the altar of our fallen veterans, and prayers in their behalf are daily sent forth from hearts full of sacred memories. Their patriotism, devotion, and deeds of heroism have been celebrated in song and story for a quarter of a century, by tongue and pen of our ablest men. Memorial structures have been erected all over the land; and we here, to-day, have the grateful satisfaction of dedicating this monument, provided by the munificence of a native-born son of the town, as a tribute of honor to the soldiers of Sutton.

The ceremonies of this occasion are now a matter of history. One thing more will make them complete. Will you all join with me in giving three rousing cheers for the donor of this monument, George Alfred Pillsbury? Now open your Sutton throats! Hip! hip! hurrah!

A benediction by Chaplain Hardy closed the exercises of a red-letter day in the history of Sutton.

PILLSBURY FREE LIBRARY,

WARNER, NEW HAMPSHIRE.

PILLSBURY FREE LIBRARY.

The Pillsbury Free Library building stands at the corner of Main and Depot streets, on a lot which was given to the town by Hon. N. G. Ordway. It is a handsome structure of pressed brick with Concord granite trimmings, and faces the north on Main street. Its dimensions are 23x48 feet, the east end being octagonal in shape; one story in height, and basement; hip roof, slated, and surmounted with copper finials and ridge roll of unique design. The main entrance on the north is an arched opening of fine hammered granite, recessed toward the door three and one half feet. Above the arch is an ornamental gable of dressed granite, resting on carved corbels, running to a point, and bearing the inscription,

PILLSBURY
FREE LIBRARY.

The height of the arch is eleven feet. Five granite steps lead to the door. The basement is well lighted on the south, and ventilated. The west end is finished for a pamphlet-room, and the furnace is in the east end. The reading-room, in the east part, is 25x20 feet, lighted in the octagonal end by four square-top windows, with a transom over each of beautiful leaded glass. On the south side of the room is a hammered stone fire-place, circular in shape, with tile hearth. A highly ornamented wood mantel, eight feet long and thirteen feet from floor to top, has in the centre of the top a finely carved frame, in which is a portrait of Mr. Pillsbury, 30x34 inches. On the right and left of the fireplace are handsomely carved ingle seats of quartered oak. The walls of the room are wainscoted to the height of seven and one half feet with panel work of quartered oak. At the left of the entrance door is a case for reference-books. The librarian's room is separated from the reading-room by a screen of two-sided panel-work and plate and leaded glasswork. In the centre of the screen is a counter, with drawers and cupboards for the librarian's use. On the south side is a small office, lighted with one window, and containing a book-case for the librarian. On the north side, access to the basement is had by an iron stair-case. A partition divides this room from the stack-room, and in the centre of it is a sliding door, 6x7½ feet, surmounted by a circular top transom of handsome leaded glass. The stack-room is 19x20 feet, and nineteen feet in height. It is lighted by eight windows with circular top, on the north and south sides, and two windows with square top and transom on the west end. The room is provided with six double and four single cherry book-cases, seven and one half feet high. The ceiling is circular in shape and handsomely frescoed. The finish is of quartered oak, and the floors of birch. It is a gem of a building. The stone- and brick-work were done by J. H. Flood, and the wood-work by E. B. Hutchinson, both of Concord.

DEDICATORY EXERCISES.

The dedicatory exercises of the Pillsbury Free Library building in Warner occurred at the town hall on Friday, October 2, 1891. The hall was filled to its utmost capacity, and on the platform were seated some of the oldest citizens of the town, the trustees of the library, the donors of site and structure, the speakers, and many invited guests. At 1 o'clock p. m., Major Samuel Davis, president of the day, called the assembly to order. Prayer was offered by Rev. Robert Bennett, pastor of the Congregational church, which was followed with a selection by Blaisdell's orchestra, of Concord, and the following opening address by Major Davis:

The world does move. The great law of the universe never lost a day. Progress is always involved in the evolutionary movement. Whether we gaze into the nebulæ of the heavens, or contemplate the spirit of God moving upon the face of the deep, we see new and beautiful things coming forth out of that which was without form, and void. It always was so; it always will be so until the perfect day.

But it is in human nature itself, in the discoveries, the arts, and the inventions of men, and in the rise and fall of nations, peoples, and civilizations—always leaving remains from which a higher line is to spring up—that we find our strongest attraction. We could have had no Greece without an Egypt in the background; no New Testament without an Old one; no Rome until the older nations and civilizations were going to decay; and without a Caesar to carry civilization inland from the Mediterranean, the continent of Europe would have been barbarous to-day. There could have been no Martin Luther in North Germany, no King Henry VIII of England, and consequently no common schools in America, in this year of our Lord. But without the common school there could be no high school, and without schools there could be no public libraries—in the popular sense.

But to come down to our own time and state. Within the memory of men now living and here to-day, within the memory of the chairman of this meeting, there was established in a large portion of the villages of the rural districts of our state some sort of a literary and scientific institution where the higher education could be obtained by the youth of our land. They were largely of the denominational kind, and their support depended very much upon the patronage of the cities in the lower part of the state and in Massachusetts; and the stage-coaches of those days were packed with pupils and their baggage as they came in at the beginning and returned at the close of the term. But the citizens of Massachusetts found out that it was cheaper and better to establish high schools at home than to send their children out of the state, and they did so. As a result, the academies of New Hampshire died a natural death, except here and there one of the stronger type; of course, it was the fittest that survived. But this left our youth, who were hungering for an education, in a bad way,—unless their parents were forehanded, which was not apt to be the case. However, the assembled wisdom of our state appreciated the situation, and gave us a high school law ourselves; and now the high school is doing the work of the academy of the past.

As time moved on, the discovery was made that we could teach our children but little at school, at most—little more than supply them with implements for work ; that something besides cramming from text-books was needed to raise our sons and daughters to the noble stature of grand manhood and womanhood. And now comes what I am going to characterize as the cap-sheaf, the crowning glory, of modern Christian civilization, the public library, which furnishes all within its reach with the means of a truly liberal education and high culture.

We hear in these days much of environment—the surroundings from which we draw the life we live, not only the physical, but the intellectual, moral, and spiritual. But what is to be the environment of the youth of Warner, of all of us ? From our schools and libraries we may draw nourishment from all the sources of knowledge in the world, and learn the upshot, the quintessence, of the wisdom of the universe ; for every age has its man, or very few men, who absorb all the learning of all the preceding ages. When I think of the higher learning and the higher environment,—and of that highest environment, which includes "the dear old spiritual work,"—and reflect upon the vast strides that have already been made in the universal march from the innocence of ignorance to the innocence of wisdom, I feel something of the glory involved in eternal knowledge and eternal existence.

The oldest library is said to have been founded at Memphis, by an Egyptian king of the Twelfth Dynasty, at the entrance of which were these words, "The healing of the soul." They have come down to us, through the corridors of time, with all their divine import; and as we look upon that staunch and enduring structure of brick and granite that stands at the corner of Main and Depot streets, many a heart will involuntarily exclaim, "The healing of the soul!" It is the munificent gift of a former resident of this town, Hon. George Alfred Pillsbury, who will now formally present it to you.

Mr. Pillsbury spoke as follows:

MR. CHAIRMAN, LADIES AND GENTLEMEN: On the first day of February, 1840, at the age of twenty-four years, I became a resident of the town of Warner, and continued to reside here until March 1, 1852. During my residence here, of about twelve years, I was engaged in active business, with the exception of one year. I came here as a clerk for Mr. John H. Pearson, who was at that time engaged in the mercantile business. In less than a year I bought out Mr. Pearson, and commenced business for myself. I brought with me less than $500; and during the eleven years I carried on business here I worked day and night to secure some of this world's goods. How well I succeeded you can judge, when I say that I took away with me less than $3,000. In 1841 I married Margaret Carleton, and brought her here. For more than half a century she has been my companion in life, and by her presence and words has ever assisted and encouraged me. Our two oldest children were born here:—the oldest, Charles A., is still living, but the other, a daughter, sleeps in the cemetery yonder.

Thus it is that my domestic and home life, as well as my business life, was really commenced here. I was at that time young and active, and full of hope for the future. And although other places, and the engrossing cares of business, have taken my time and attention since I left Warner, nevertheless the twelve years of my early life spent here have made this place and its people dear to me. I have ever taken a lively interest in all that has tended to the prosperity of Warner, and I have never forgotten the confidence reposed in me by its citizens, and the marks of appreciation it has bestowed upon me. The citizens of Warner have given me the highest honors within their gift. Both Mrs. Pillsbury and I became very much attached to the people of Warner, and during the long interval of time which has elapsed since we left this town, our love and esteem have continued, and will continue during the years to come. As we greet you to-day, a feeling of sadness comes over us, as we call to mind our friends of fifty years ago. Here and there, scattered through this audience, we see the face of an old-time friend; but the marks of time are there, and the whitening locks recall that we are growing old and that eternity is near. How these intervening years have thinned our ranks! Most of those with whom we used to associate have passed the border of this life, and we shall see them no more in this world. Friends, good and true, whose hearts were true to us in the long ago, crowd upon our thoughts, and in the joy of this occasion we would not forget them, but would ever keep alive their memory. But what joy does it give us to see present, to-day, so many of those whom we knew so well fifty years ago, and whose friendship we have so highly valued during these years. God bless them all, and may their last days be their best days.

I have always considered Warner one of the best towns in this state, all things considered, and especially since the railroad was built here. It is an excellent agricultural town; it has always been liberal in the support of its churches and common schools; its standard of morality has always been high; and its citizens have been thrifty, honest, and industrious. I can see no reason why it should not become one of the wealthiest and most sterling towns in this state. In my opinion, however, it needs more push and enterprise, and in these days of sharp competition, a community, like an individual, in order to succeed, must have enterprise and enthusiasm, or the younger blood of other localities will pass by it. I wish you had more Governor Ordways to build mountain roads, and to help make other improvements, in order to attract people of wealth to become its citizens. I can see no reason why Warner should not become one of the best resorts in the state for summer boarders. Communication with all parts of the country by railroad is easy; no town in the state has better roads and highways for pleasure-driving; its scenery is beautiful. Where can be found pleasanter places for pleasant drives or residences than are to be found on the Tory Hill road, on Burnt Hill, on Pumpkin Hill, or on the Mink Hills, to say nothing of the beautiful road from Bradford to Hopkinton, passing through Stevensville, by Roby's Corner, to Waterloo, Warner Village, Warner Lower Village, and so on to Hopkinton? I understand that your neighboring town of New London, the past season, had more than twelve hundred visitors during the summer months. If that be so, it seems to me that with the same effort Warner ought to have at least three thousand summer residents. The northern part of the state is getting rich from this source. Millions of money ought to be brought into New Hampshire by its summer boarders, and with proper effort Warner could secure its share. But few towns in the state will compare with it in all that goes to make an attractive place for permanent or temporary residence. I hope the good people of Warner will seriously consider this matter, and at once take active measures to advance the town along this line.

I have for the past twenty years been interested in one industry that has yielded a good income, so that I have been enabled to accumulate what I hope will be enough to support me and mine the few years we shall remain here, and possibly a little more; and so, about two years ago, I began to consider whether or not it would be well to remember in some substantial way the people of Warner, in consideration of the honors they had conferred upon me while a resident here. In considering this matter, it occurred to me that perhaps the gift of a library building would be as beneficial and lasting as anything I could do, knowing, as I did, that by the munificence of one of your former residents a high school had been established here. That was a noble gift, and will be a lasting benefit to all the people of this town and vicinity.

While thinking over this matter, and before I had reached a final conclusion, Governor Ordway happened accidentally to call upon me at my office in Minneapolis. I told him what I had been thinking of, and asked him whether he thought such a gift would be acceptable to the people of Warner. He assured me that he had no doubt that such a gift would be appreciated, and at once said if I concluded to erect such a building he would cheerfully give the lot upon which the building should stand, or, if preferred, he would sell the land to me at a very low price. I also communicated with others of your citizens, and became satisfied that such a building would be very acceptable. With these assurances, I at once decided to erect such a building. I employed Mr. Harry W. Jones, of Minneapolis, a very competent and skilful architect, to prepare plans for the same. These plans, when made, were laid before some of your leading citizens, and were by them approved. When it came to a final location of the building, I found there was some difference of opinion, and I must confess that at one time I rather favored another site. In the spring of 1890, I came here and looked at the several sites that had been named, and came to the conclusion that the site where the building now stands, all things considered, was the most desirable of any that could be obtained, and at once informed Governor Ordway of my conclusion, and told him that so far as I was concerned, and so far as I could learn the sentiment of the people of Warner, they would be well satisfied to accept his generous offer. I suggested that he give a deed of the said land to the town of Warner. He at once did so, and the deed has been in the hands of Mr. A. P. Davis for more than one year. I am of the opinion that no mistake has been made as to the location. And so the building was erected. I have endeavored to have constructed a building as thoroughly made and as conveniently arranged as was possible, without regard to cost. I think no building in the state of the same size has been more thoroughly made, or at a greater cost for its size. The contractors have fulfilled their contracts to my entire satisfaction.

I had supposed, from what I had read in your local newspaper (I am a regular subscriber to it, and read it with interest), that you had quite a library, and needed only a good building to put the library into. It seems that I was mistaken. You had only a small library, which was located in your high-school building, and I understood that some who had been interested in that library were opposed to its being moved to the new building, and that others did not wish to press the matter against the opinion of those who had been associated with them in its care. This being the case, it looked as though a building had been erected without books to put in it. At the time it was decided to erect this library building, my wife expressed a desire to leave a sum of money to the town, the interest of which should forever go towards sustaining the library. When it was learned that possibly there would be no books to go into the new building, my wife concluded that she would invest the sum that she expected to leave, at the present time, in books. My two sons, Charles A. and Fred C., also offered to contribute something towards supplying the new building with books. Competent persons, in whom we had the utmost confidence, were employed to select some four or five thousand volumes of the most suitable books for a library for a town the size of Warner. Some three thousand books have already been bought, and are now in the care of Miss Mary B. Harris, to be, by her and her sister, Miss Amanda B. Harris, prepared and catalogued ready for use. Other books will be selected, and it is hoped and expected that by the first of January next some five thousand volumes will be placed upon the shelves of the building.

And now, Mr. President, please accept from me, as a gift to the town of Warner, this library building. I now deliver to you its keys. And in behalf of my wife, Margaret Carleton Pillsbury, and my two sons, Charles Alfred Pillsbury and Fred Carleton Pillsbury, I also present, for the library, the books which have already been purchased and the others that are to be purchased and placed upon the library shelves. Will you please accept them, too? In closing, it is my wish, and the wish of those whom I to-day represent in thus formally presenting these gifts to you, that all the people of Warner, old and young, the rich and the poor alike, may realize therefrom all the benefits that a free public library can give; and we trust that our most ardent anticipations of the benign influences of the library during the future years and upon the coming generations will be fully realized.

Hon. Nehemiah G. Ordway, in presenting the site on which the library building stood, said,—

Mr. Chairman: It affords me great pleasure to be able to contribute in a small degree to the munificent gift which my lifelong friend, Mr. Pillsbury, has bestowed upon the present and future generations of Warner in this gem of a public library building. The rarest jewels are not valued for their size, but for their beauty and fineness.

I am proud to be the donor of this historic hotel building lot and grounds to my native town, to be kept forever for the public uses to which they are now being dedicated. This central location, in our now prosperous Centre Village, was early improved, by Nathan S. Colby, Nathan Walker, Webster B. Davis, and others, for hotel purposes; and my own ambition to give the public a modernized hotel at this gateway to grand old Kearsarge mountain went up in the flames which swept away with the hotel the necessary adjuncts—trees and shade. I therefore cheerfully, like one of old, have added my mite to Mr. Pillsbury's priceless gift to the whole people of Warner.

I have been familiar with this village for more than fifty years. I well remember when Mr. Pillsbury, the young merchant from Sutton, brought his bride to our village; and later on I recall the bright face of a nervy boy, Charles A., who made the raisin kegs, candy cans, and such things as boys love, rattle all around the old Robertson store, giving us a foretaste of the way he has since shaken up the old milling systems of the West by the adoption of new methods, until the name of C. A. Pillsbury & Co. is as well known in all the produce exchanges of the world as is that of Jay Gould on the stock exchanges.

To have been the parents of such a son, and to cheerfully return to the scenes of their early life for the purpose of erecting such monuments of their generosity for the alleviation of suffering and for the diffusion of such a rich store of useful knowledge, are privileges and honors which few will be enabled to enjoy in this life, and they have the promise that in the life hereafter "God loves cheerful givers."

My friends and fellow-citizens, we can hardly fully estimate the advantages of this free library, filled with thousands of the rarest and richest books to be found in this great country—books suited to all ages and all conditions in life, from the lisping little prattler to the ripe scholar, editor, and historian. As my memory carries me back to my boyhood days, when I learned to spell and write the names of the different commodities under the tutelage of my venerable friend, Robert Thompson, in his store, and, later on, when I had to part with my highly prized silver watch to pay the expenses of a single term of the high school at Bradford, how much would I have given for the present privileges of the Warner high school and this free library.

As I look around this splendid audience to-day, and note the presence of so many of our old and venerable citizens, I think I voice their general sentiments when I say that however much of success those of us have achieved who have struggled up and along life's journey without these privileges, we cannot relieve ourselves of the responsibility of giving those who are soon to take our places educational advantages which will meet the requirements of the present time.

The small sums we are called to pay in our annual tax-list for these free, higher-class educational institutions will be much less in the future than ignorance, poverty, and crime would load upon us through the poor-house, courts, and prisons. The library benefits all classes; and those of us who are passing the plain or the down-hill of life will find solace in perusing this rare collection of books during the long winter evenings, and when disease and decrepitude confine us at home. In a word, what we pay for the economical care of this beautiful and richly appointed library, which will stand the shock of time for ages, is especially for the benefit of every tax-payer and his family; while the large amount we pay for schools is for the exclusive benefit of those who pay no tax, *the children*, but to whom we owe a debt which all should be willing cheerfully to pay.

It is true that the late census does not give Warner as many people as were here when I was a boy; but if I could foot up the number of our sons and daughters whom I know to have gone to the great cities and western prairies with the view of securing a competency, and then returning to some spot, dear to them and their childhood, for at least a summer home, I could easily show you that the present Warner, with nine miles of railroad running six daily trains, receiving passengers at seven stations, and receiving and delivering mails at six post-offices, has more friends and more resources to draw upon in an emergency than the town ever had. That its educational and literary attainments are far ahead of any town in the state having the same enumerated population will not seriously be questioned. Although I have helped to build up in the West, I am loyal to and proud of my native town. I love its mountains, down whose sides the clear, health-giving, and sparkling water frets its way to the valleys, to be utilized for new industries with improved machinery operated by educated intelligence. I admire its beautiful scenery, its fine roads, and its variegated foliage.

In conclusion, my friends, allow me to urge upon you to make this day of our friend's benefaction a red-letter day for all coming time; and let us resolve that hereafter we will use our best efforts to induce each and every present and former resident of the town to keep its name and fame for the public good, above all self-interests, and see to it that in the future, as in the past, such examples of public spirit and improvement may prevail that we shall leave many monuments to show that we have not lived in vain.

Albert P. Davis, Esq., chairman of the board of trustees of the library, accepted the same in these words:

MR. CHAIRMAN, MR. PILLSBURY: It would seem an idle use of words for me to say that the final and official act of accepting, at your generous hands, this magnificent gift to the people of Warner that you have just formally presented, affords pleasure to me and to those for whom I speak— pleasure and satisfaction beyond the power of language to express; and I am sure I voice the united sentiment of our people in saying that we return you our sincere and earnest thanks for this beautiful, rich, and artistic library building, and for the generous gift of books. Our hearts overflow with gratitude. We are your debtors, always. It is said, "It is more blessed to give than to receive." If that be true, and if the pleasure the giving affords you is equal to the gratification afforded us as the beneficiaries of your princely benefaction, you must be happy indeed. In behalf of the trustees of the Pillsbury Free Library chosen by the unanimous vote of the town, and in behalf of all the people of Warner, I accept this noble institution of learning, with all that it implies of legal obligation on the part of the town, and of personal and official obligation on the part of the board of trustees, and of duty on the part of the people; and I give you our promise, for ourselves and our children and our children's children forever, that we will religiously guard it as a sacred trust. Again, in the name of all the people of Warner. I thank you, Mr. Pillsbury, most heartily.

To our distinguished fellow-townsman, Governor Ordway, for the generous and kindly gift of the land on which the library stands, and for his early and always earnest interest in behalf of the Pillsbury Free Library, we return our thanks, assuring him that we appreciate the noble and generous spirit that induced him to make this donation of valuable land to further the purposes of Mr. Pillsbury. Permit me to say to, and of, our respected fellow-citizen, that you have done yourself great honor, and your native town a generous service, in the gift you have made. We accept the title-deed from you with pleasure, assuring you that the town will, along with the building and the library, ever guard it and its interests with a watchful and jealous eye. Future generations will hold in grateful memory all who have kindly contributed to the consummation of the work of founding this institution.

Having said so much in grateful recognition of the treasures we this day receive at the hands of our friends, you will permit me to indulge in a few practical reflections that this auspicious event seems to suggest. The founding of this free library marks the beginning of a new era in the history of Warner, second in importance to no other, and co-equal with that of the founding of our free high school. Indeed, I may, with absolute fairness, couple the Simonds Free High School with the

Pillsbury Free Library as twin blessings, each the counterpart of the other. When the town voted, by a unanimous vote, and with an enthusiasm unprecedented in the history of Warner town-meetings, to accept this last great and crowning blessing, it completed the work so well begun two decades ago. Providence has been exceedingly kind and partial to us, as a town, in so ordering events that we are permitted to enjoy the privileges which these institutions of learning afford us and coming generations forever, for few rural towns possess two such public institutions. It is also fortunate that these great blessings came at a time when the men of Warner were wise enough to know and accept a good thing when it was offered them, even though it involved slight taxation. There have been times when they would have been refused.

Warner has taken a new departure. She henceforth discards her dead past, with all its local and personal quarrels and dead issues, and turns her face sunward, to a bright and promising future. Let those who would hinder and obstruct her upward course stand from under. The people have decreed it. The will of the people is omnipotent. Warner is now in the flood-tide of prosperity, financially, socially, and industrially. This satisfactory condition is traceable to well known causes, and has not come about from any accidental cause or purely fortunate circumstance, independent of the universal law of cause and effect. It is always true that "God helps them that help themselves." The greatest of philosophers said, of the fortunes of men,—

> There is a tide in the affairs of men,
> Which, taken at the flood, leads on to fortune;
> Omitted, all the voyage of their life
> Is bound in shallows and in miseries.

Communities are no more the creatures of fortuitous circumstances than are individuals. Rather, we are creatures of opportunity and not of circumstance. That person, as well as that town, is wise, who, seeing the opportunity, improves it.

When the high school was offered us, it was a tide in the destiny of the town, which, if not accepted, would most effectually have "bound our voyage in shallows and in miseries." Fortunately our people were wise, and gladly accepted Mr. Simonds's noble and generous gift. Again: When in the course of events the Pillsbury Free Library was offered us, came our second tide and our second great opportunity to decide; and, by reason of that wise decision, the town has taken its place in the van of healthy, prosperous, and enterprising New Hampshire towns. These two fortunate events in the history of Warner, and the good sense of the people called upon to act with respect to them, have fixed the status of our town and given her an enviable reputation. Let us, upon whom now rest the responsibilities of life, see to it that we realize all the benefits possible from these events, for it is true, as stated by Mr. Pillsbury in the correspondence that led to his generous gift, "With the Simonds Free High School and a Free Public Library, free to all the people, Warner would be one of the most attractive towns in New Hampshire in which to make a home."

These rare institutions in rural towns ought to attract to us those seeking educational privileges of a high order, in a community as pure and healthy and vigorous as the breezes that forever fan the brow of our own Kearsarge.

Then, too, we count ourselves exceedingly fortunate because this free library places us in line with the advanced educational spirit of this age, that demands a higher and broader education for our boys and girls than that of the generations past. This is emphatically the intellectual age of the world. The iron age is past; that of gold, nearly. Mind is superior to matter, brains to muscle, and intellect and culture to gold and sordid greed of gain. A free library, too, is a necessary part of our system of popular education. The free l'brary is but another advance step to round out to completion the people's common-school system. It is the process of evolution in the development and growth of that institution of our fathers.

Horace Mann, the father of the present system of popular education that has placed Massachusetts at the head of American states, said, many years ago, that "A public library in a town is as necessary as the little red school-house." The desire for knowledge is strong with the masses. The good of society demands that that sentiment should be encouraged. The free library affords the exact stimulus required. Books, magazines, and newspapers are no longer a luxury in American homes. They are found everywhere, as well in the humble cottage of the average American laborer as in the stately mansion of the rich. In consequence of this growing thirst for knowledge on the part of the "plain people," as defined by Lincoln, our state, taking Massachusetts for her pattern, at the last session of the legislature passed an act entitled "An act to promote the establishment and efficiency of free public libraries," by which towns showing a desire to establish free libraries by making small annual appropriations are entitled to state aid. The next step in our system will be the enactment of a law obliging towns to make these annual appropriations as a part of the system. Why not? It is but an enlargement of the compulsory features of our present law, which the law of self-preservation has forced us to enact.

As a nation, we have become the dumping-ground of the ignorance and superstition of the Old World. After one hundred years of national life, we cannot view with indifference this invasion of our free institutions, and we are enabled to realize the value of schools, churches, and libraries, and to appreciate the profound statesmanship of Washington when he said, in his farewell message to his countrymen,—"It is substantially true that virtue or morality is a mainspring of popular government. Who that is a sincere friend of it can look with indifference upon attempts to shake the foundation of the fabric? Promote, then, as an object of primary importance, institutions for the general diffusion of knowledge. In proportion as the structure of government gives force to public opinion, it is essential that public opinion should be enlightened."

This is sound doctrine, in the enforcement of

which lie the safety of our people and the perpetuity of our free institutions. It was the same enlightened statesmanship that inspired our fathers to declare, in our New Hampshire Bill of Rights, that "a frequent recurrence to the fundamental principles of the constitution, and a constant adherence to justice, moderation, temperance, industry, frugality, and all the social virtues, are indispensably necessary to preserve the blessings of liberty and free government." At no time since the founding of the Plymouth colony have these precepts been more valuable than now.

You will agree with me that any institution that inculcates these great and sublime doctrines, that are so well intended to keep alive forever the fires that burn on the altar of our liberties, is deserving the patriotic support of every good citizen. It is because this free library will help to inculcate these great truths to our children in all coming time, and because it will make them better, and therefore happier, because more intelligent and more patriotic, that every true son and daughter of Warner rejoices over the Pillsbury Free Library. True to the patriotic instincts that inspire love of country in every patriotic heart, we join our rejoicings to-day over the completion of this institution, proud of the rising fortunes of our town, of the increased prosperity and happiness of her people, and of the rich blessings the budding future presents.

Charles Sumner described our school-houses as "the gates of knowledge, which are also the shining gates of civilization." The common school is the richest and most priceless legacy we have inherited from the founders of our New England civilization. It comes to us charged with the condition to transmit it unimpaired to our children. This is a solemn responsibility. As it was their duty to conceive and establish, it is ours to inherit and preserve and transmit. If the teachings of nearly three centuries of the struggles of humanity to liberate itself from the bondage of the past teach anything, it is that a people to be happy must be virtuous and intelligent. Our fathers realized the truth of this, for they fled from the worst conditions of ignorance, bigotry, and intolerance the world ever saw. To avoid an ultimate like condition in America, they established the church and the school side by side—twin conditions by which liberty might be preserved and happiness secured. They made no mistake, for they have made New England what she is—the home of liberty, education, learning, and intelligence. A sweet New England poet has happily expressed the idea in these lines:

> "Yet on her rocks and on her sands
> And winter hills the school-house stands;
> And what the rugged soil denies,
> The harvest of the mind supplies,—
>
> "Nor heeds the skeptic's puny hands,
> While by the school the church spire stands;
> Nor fears the blinded bigots' rule,
> While near the church spire stands the school."

To-day the gates of knowledge and of civilization are the school-house and the free library.

Thoughtful American observers, who love their country more than anything else, agree that this grand system of popular, free, and unsectarian education is endangered by this foreign invasion, and its influence in politics and at the ballot-box. Let it be the pride and joy of every native American, whatever our differences politically, that our common school is our common birthright and family heritage, and the common mother of us all, to whom we owe a common loyalty and a common love.

To the men and women of Warner given to literary pursuits, the literati of Warner, this is a red-letter day indeed. To them this library means much, for it will afford first-class facilities for thorough reading in all departments of literature,—historical, biographical, and scientific. To the girls and boys of the town who hunger and thirst for knowledge without the means of satisfying their wants, this free library will be of incalculable worth, for it opens to them a vista of pleasure and unalloyed happiness well worthy the envy of those not thus signally blessed. "The finished garden to the view its vistas open, and its alleys green." To the few who have been hoping with faint hope and praying with little faith, who have long waited for this glorious day, I tender my special congratulations over hopes realized, prayers answered, and labors rewarded.

In conclusion, Mr. Chairman, as expressive of the pleasure we all feel, permit me to say, in the language of a distinguished American author, who said of his books, with which he was in love,—

"Let us thank God for books. When I consider what some books have done for the world and what they are doing, how they keep up our hope, awaken new courage and faith, soothe pain, give an ideal life to those whose homes are hard and cold, bind together distant ages and foreign lands, create new worlds of beauty, bring down truths from heaven, I give eternal blessings for this gift, and pray that we may use it aright and abuse it not."

A selection by the orchestra followed, after which United States Senator William E. Chandler was introduced as the orator of the day.

SENATOR CHANDLER'S ORATION.

The time allotted to me will be given to an ascription of thanks to the donors of the attractive Pillsbury Free Library, to the assertion of the transcendent importance to a republic of education and culture, and to congratulations to the citizens most interested in the library upon the superior advantages which they enjoy as residents of one of the best of towns in our beloved state.

The library building stands, as it should, on ample and sure foundations. The land on which it has been built is the free gift to the town of Warner from one of its native citizens. Mr. Ordway was born upon the nearest slope of the Mink Hills. Possessing only those opportunities for education and advancement in life which in those days lay before the humblest of Warner's children, he made the utmost of his chances. By the most untiring and sleepless industry, and by patience and endeavor unremitting in the face of all obstacles, he made himself one of the foremost men of his town. Moving to Concord, he advanced easily and quickly to the front rank of the citizens of the capital. Called to Washington as a public official, he disbursed millions of public money during the long period of twelve years without a default or complaint, and he became the trusted associate and adviser of the highest leaders of the nation. Sent by President Hayes to our greatest territory as its governor, he perfected its organization and prepared it for statehood under circumstances of trial and difficulty; and although he was beset by many and powerful foes, who were the enemies of good government as well, he maintained his integrity and high repute to a triumphant conclusion. No one locality has ever wholly engrossed his limitless energies. In Dakota, in the District of Columbia, and in New Hampshire he has engaged in innumerable enterprises, public and private; and wherever he has been he has always wished to do his part in every good work. During this season, while improving his farm and beautifying his summer home, he has rejoiced that he embraced the opportunity of aiding this project of a free library by donating the one appropriate site therefor, the title to which has passed to his native town with his earnest wish and high hope that the institution now inaugurated may be fruitful in blessings to a community which has never failed to engage his warmest affections.

Seven cities contended for the honor of some

of Homer's fame. Mr. Pillsbury can be proudly claimed by two towns and two cities. In Sutton he was born; Warner was the home of his youthful struggles; Concord, the scene of his manhood's labors; and Minneapolis sees the full fruition of his noble life. In his personal presence it is becoming to speak of him with some reserve, and to limit carefully the words of eulogy. Yet, having known and watched him well through all my life, and being deeply interested personally in the welfare of one of the towns and one of the cities which are profiting by his benevolence, I must be allowed to utter with freedom the language of truthfulness, not in a recital of the incidents of his career, but in a just judgment of his character and achievements.

Mr. Pillsbury, from his earliest youth, has possessed in a high degree the industry, energy, and persistency which were common traits of the men of New Hampshire born during the first third of the present century, when our rigorous climate, stubborn lands, and undeveloped resources made marked success in life impossible to the indolent, to the slothful, or to the faint-hearted. Hard and unremitting toil, day in and day out, was the lot of the promising boys of those days. Such schooling as the town gave was not neglected, but attendance was work and not play. "Whatsoever thy hand findeth to do, do it with thy might," was the rule which guided the four Pillsbury boys under the direction of their father, Captain John Pillsbury, who had a living and "a good name which is better than riches" to earn for himself and his family, under the severe conditions which then prevailed in the deep woods and scant meadows and on the rocky hillsides of the secluded town of Sutton. To these very conditions, doubtless—also to inheritance, probably—Mr. Pillsbury is indebted for that disposition to do things, that forcefulness and indefatigability, which have given him such far reaching and abundant success that he is now entitled to look with just complacency, and to rest with supreme satisfaction, upon the work which he has wrought during his journey of life.

Four distinguishing traits are prominent in the character of the subject of these remarks. Good sense, common sense, has ever been present with him, keeping him from mistakes, and enabling him to say and do the right thing at the right time. Good nature, affability, manifested in every relation of life, making him courteous, gentle, and patient with all his fellow-creatures, has made his own pathway easier, and that of those nearest and dearest to him happier for his presence and association.

Integrity, including truthfulness, honesty, and honor in all his dealings with his fellow-men, has always controlled his private and public life, and no imputation to the contrary has ever been made by any person, on any occasion, or in any form.

Above all else, he has been and is a man of religious convictions, deep-seated and sincere, unconcealed but unostentatious, pervading and guiding every movement of his existence. Accounting himself as an heir of immortality, from his youth upward he has endeavored, as God has given him strength and opportunity, so to live his long life among men as not to be wholly unworthy of the better country, even the heavenly.

Such being Mr. Pillsbury's prominent traits of character, which, while they do not always secure great worldly success to their possessors, certainly are quite likely to promote it, he has achieved positions and honors and riches such as fall to the lot of only a few men, even in our highly favored and prosperous country. Withal, it has pleased him to enter into works of benevolence, many of which have been secret, and some of which have necessarily come to public view. He has not been alone in his good deeds, but has been joined by his brother, Governor John S. Pillsbury, who has given to Sutton a memorial hall, soon to be dedicated, and by his remarkably capable and successful son, Mr. Charles A. Pillsbury. It may be said, I think, and said because it is just and true, of this family, which had its origin among our granite hills, migrated to the great West, and achieved wealth and power and distinction, that all its members have deserved their prosperity, and are worthily performing all their duties to their fellow-men.

Mr. Pillsbury has made various donations in my native city of Concord. His latest is the Margaret Pillsbury General Hospital, named after his respected wife, who seconds him in all his good works. This hospital is one of the noblest of charities; and I take this public occasion to thank Mr. Pillsbury for his complete and timely benefaction. Only a few days ago was unveiled the monument given by him to the town of Sutton to commemorate the soldiers who went thence to give their lives in the greatest and noblest war of which history makes record, which was fought to suppress the slaveholders' rebellion, to save the union of these states, and to make America wholly and forever free.

To-day, moreover, Mr. Pillsbury presents to the town of Warner this beautiful and commodious free library building. It is a most appropriate gift, and is most gratefully accepted.

To you, sir, I take pride in saying that the gratitude of this people goes out to you in unstinted measure. Not only are you thanked for your liberality by those now living, but you may be sure that many generations yet to live in the town of your earlier strivings, when they assemble in the precincts of this enduring edifice and enjoy its advantages, will recall your name with thanks and blessings. Heaven has already generously lengthened your days, with health and strength unimpaired. May your life be prolonged far into the future, and may the best of God's rewards belong to you forever and ever.

The importance of a free public library in every considerable village of the United States cannot be overestimated. The government of this country is that of a republic. It is the greatest republic of the world. Here we are trying the momentous experiment whether mankind is capable of self-government. The whole world is looking on. If we fail, republican governments everywhere will go down, and despotisms will take their places. We have passed safely through many tests since our fathers in 1776 rebelled against the tyranny of

England and established our nation. We justly resisted foreign aggression in the War of 1812. We immensely enlarged our boundaries in 1846, and for that purpose successfully waged an unjust war with Mexico. We subdued the most formidable rebellion which ever, in the history of the world, uplifted its head against established government, and in that war we tore up and extinguished the curse of human chattel slavery; and to-day the United States are enjoying the highest prosperity they have ever known, with the complete apparent safety and stability of our government.

All this is hopeful and encouraging. Yet with pride and prosperity there can be seen new perils. I will enumerate some of them without elaborating. There is danger from the existence of two races of different color, each entitled to go to the ballot-box; from the influx and naturalization of ignorant foreigners; from degraded and vicious voters, native and foreign, in our great cities; from the antagonisms between capital, and laborers with ballots in their hands; from the prevalence of both enormous wealth and extreme poverty; from the arrogance of plutocratic corporation monopolies on the one side, and the desperation of socialists and anarchists on the other; and from the corruption and intimidation of voters from various causes. I am hopeful, but anxious, and believe that no pains should be spared to avert dangers and strengthen our republican form of government.

It is agreed on every side that all the greatest dangers to republicanism arise from, or are increased by, illiteracy; and that the education of the masses of the people should be promoted by all apt and possible means. It is a trite subject, that of popular education, but it is the indispensable basis of our American liberty. If we can decrease illiteracy and secure education, and that intelligence concerning public affairs which in these days of books and newspapers follows education, we can save and perpetuate our free institutions. But if illiteracy and ignorance are to gain upon us, and education is not to be widely diffused through the masses of the people, into all our families, and among all our voters, the republic may at some crisis be destroyed. The new republic of Brazil, the other Central and South American republics, and even the republic of France, will, in my opinion, not be permanent unless each nation erects and maintains as the chief bulwark of its liberties a system of common schools substantially like our own, and bases its hopes of endurance upon widely diffused and universal popular education.

That system of common schools is firmly established in the United States, and we must cherish it as the most precious safeguard of our liberties. We must strengthen it on every side, and must resist all attempts, whether open or insidious, to break it down by the substitution of private schools advocated on the false plea of the necessity of religious instruction. Let our children, of all classes, races, and religious denominations, be given the rudiments of education in unsectarian schools; and let their religious opinions be inculcated or formed as may happen in a nation whose constitutions declare that the governments shall "make no law respecting an establishment of religion, or prohibiting the free exercise thereof."

Let us continue to supplement the common schools with the best possible high schools, technical schools, agricultural schools, colleges, and universities, liberally endowed by wealthy and generous citizens "willing to communicate." Let us rejoice in the public libraries which in recent years are springing into existence over all the land, beautifying our villages by their tasteful architecture, inviting our youths away from hurtful resorts, and inspiring them with zeal for the highest culture, furnishing our citizens with full knowledge of all public events, and fitting them for the wise performance of their most important duties of citizenship, those of voters and rulers in the leading republic of the world.

Citizens of Warner: You are this day highly blessed in lacking nothing necessary to popular education in your midst. Your public schools are good, and there is only needed more effort to assist the attendance of children from some of the remoter farm-houses. Many years ago a free high school, now noted for its excellence, and attracting scholars from the surrounding towns, was given to you by Mr. and Mrs. Franklin Simonds, who on this occasion should be especially and gratefully remembered. Now comes to crown the work the Pillsbury Free Library. Surely the lines have fallen to you in pleasant places. It is easy to decry our mountain state in favor of more fertile regions and milder climes, but they who go out from these hillsides to seek their fortunes turn back again to their childhood homes with gratitude and intense desire, and they tell you that not elsewhere than here can they so rejoice in the consciousness of existence. Our Kearsarge mountain gives its blessings as freely as that lofty peak of which New England's great poet sung:

> "For health comes sparkling in the streams
> From cool Chocorua stealing.
> There's iron in our northern winds;
> Our pines are trees of healing."

Thus, with natural advantages unsurpassed by any other of our rural towns; with public-spirited citizens supplying needed benefits otherwise unattainable; a prosperous, temperate, moral, and religious community,—you can assuredly this day felicitate yourselves that you are the fortunate possessors of the very best gifts which God vouchsafes, during this earthly pilgrimage, to the children of men.

After a cornet solo by Mr. Arthur F. Nevers, of Blaisdell's orchestra, Fred Myron Colby, poet of the day, was introduced, and read the following poem:

> In days of old there stood 'neath Attic skies
> A temple reared by cunning hands, and wise.
> With pillared hall and portico it rose
> Upon the heights, the wonder of both friends and foes.
> The sailor, coming in o'er slumbering seas,
> Saw far aloft, amid the sunshine and the breeze,
> The shining roofs of Nike Apteros,
> Called "The Temple of Wingless Victory," because

Erected to commemorate great Kimon's victory
Over the Persian foe beside the foaming sea.
No other fane in all Athenian story
Had ever half the grace or half the glory
Worn by this fair model of the builder's art,
Of Athens' greatness a symbol and a part.
For ages upon the Acropolis it stood
Looking down on " Violet City," plain, and wood,
Its white Ionian columns rising fair
Above the dust and din, in thin, pellucid air.
And all those lofty ones, so great in story,
Who trod these streets and waysides hoary,
Passed up the height beneath its portico
To worship or to dream, midst weal and woe,—
The statesman and the scholar, the warriors wearing
 bays;
The heroes and the victors, and the singers of sweet lays;
Young children and fair women, and laborers swart with
 toil,
The humble and the lowly from all the Attic soil.
They thronged within its shadow, or dreamed beneath its
 roof;
Not one but loved the ideal temple, and never held aloof.
Honored it was by mortals, and the dreaded gods reigned
 there
In the shining temple of Nike Apteros the fair.

This is our temple of Nike Apteros,
Built, like that of Athens, for a worthy cause:
To be the pride and glory of our town,
So that future ages, glancing down
The aisles of time with reverent eyes,
Shall see how we, beneath New England skies,
Built in the old time for posterity.
It is a temple of wingless victory
For him who founded this library grand
To be a sign and symbol through the land;

And generations yet unborn shall bless
Him who with generous hand this largess
Gave. Greater than Athens' victorious son's
Shall be his fame, and the weight of marble tons
Engraved with gold and skill shall not outweigh
The gratitude we tender him to-day.
May his years be rounded out like those
Of the ancient patriarch, and each one be
As fair and sweet as 't is full of charity.
Well and wisely has he built, as all men know,
And this shall all the future ages show.
This temple to learning and to poesy
Shall stand when we are dead, and honored be;
A grander victory it shall proclaim
Than that which graced the proud Athenian's name,—
The victory of mind. Its hosts are gods
Indeed, but gentler deities than those whose nods
Held in grim fear the men of that old time.
They are gods of truth, of reason, and of rhyme;
And this, their treasure-house of garnered thought,
Shall shine with light from distant ages brought.
Here men shall all the springs of truth explore,
And "hold communion with the minds of yore."
No blind and senseless worshippers are they
Who bend before this shrine to dream and pray.

The vistas of the future open wide before my gaze,
And I see a countless army marching up the dusty ways;
The echoes of their footsteps sound along the time-worn
    floor,
As they fill the library chambers, as they throng around
    the door,
And they crowd with reverent faces by these book-shelves
    dim and old,
Laden with volumes musty, but precious as fine gold,—
Open the pages, wide and luminous, filled with historic
    lore,

Scan the thoughts of poets, scholars, till they can read no more.
But the thronging never ceases: still the crowd comes pouring in,—
The scholar and the dreamer worn by midnight vigils thin:
The schoolboy fresh and rosy, the housewife from her toil:
The man of wealth and leisure, the tiller of the soil;—
They gather here of every age, to bow at Wisdom's shrine,
And "gleaning from the storied page," make their dull lives divine.
Some linger over Shakespeare, others o'er Gibbon's stately page;
Some seek for truth in Plato, some study a more modern sage.
The music of Tasso's glowing lines, of Byron's burning lays,
Give sweetness to the night-times and beauty to the days;
The godlike verse of Homer will have its worshippers,
And Chaucer's nightingale still through the foliage stirs.
We smell the golden daffodils in Herrick's garden fair,
And Browning still will haunt us from 'midst Venetia's glare;
The tale of sad Granada as told by Irving's pen,
And Parkman's graphic stories of his historic men.
Each, each will have its readers, and each be garnered o'er,
Year after year by those who love the past with all its wealth of lore.
And so they'll gather ever to drink from Learning's stream,
At the Pillsbury Free Library, the temple of their dream.

> A temple fair of knowledge, long may this building
> stand
> To be the scholar's Mecca, a beacon in the land:
> And while we love the temple, and ever guard the same,
> We'll not forget the gratitude we owe the Pillsbury
> name.

Following the poem was music, and remarks by the following gentlemen:

REMARKS OF HON. JOHN EATON.

The solid and fit character of the library building this day dedicated accords with the abiding and worthy end which it is to promote. Over its door may well be written the inscription found over the entrance to the library of ancient Thebes, —"Medicine for the soul."

It deserves profound gratitude and the best use. Its location here has a further value from the fact that your town and village enjoy the benefits of the Simonds Free High School. Both should make residence here more desirable, increase the skill of industry, and add value to real estate. They will be coöperative workers in the education of men and women. People are known by the institutions they cherish. Carlisle declares that the true university of these days is a collection of books. Bacon observes that libraries are the shrines where all the relics of ancient saints, full of true virtue —and that without delusion or imposture—repose. Byron sang, "A drop of ink may make a million think." Books multiply this power. Schlegel, the German philosopher, declares that "Literature is the voice that gives expression to the human intellect." Whipple calls books "the light-houses on the sea of time." Says Cicero, "They are the food of youth, the delight of age, the ornament of prosperity, the refuge and comfort of adversity." Says Milton, "A good book is the precious life-blood of a master-spirit, embalmed and treasured up on purpose for a life beyond." Old Ben Jonson sang,

> "When I would know thee, my thought looks
> Upon thy well made choice of friends and books."

Avoid a foul book as you would small-pox or the companionship of crime. The poison of bad literature is wide-spread. No miasma is more deadly. The best preventive and antidote yet found is a taste for good reading. Samuel Johnson, author of the dictionary, says,—"Books have a secret influence on the understanding. We cannot at pleasure obliterate ideas. He that reads books of science, though without any desire for improvement, will grow more knowing. He that reads moral or religious treatises will imperceptibly advance in goodness. But to get the most out of books, we must see to it that our reading be wrought into our living." Napoleon was wont to say, "My hand is near my head." His act followed closely on his thought. Read not to contradict or to confute, nor to believe and take for granted, nor to find fault, but to weigh and consider. Samuel Johnson affirms that first principles are found in books which real life must test. The administration of libraries is fast becoming a learned profession. Colleges aspire to professorships of books. A librarian may shape the reading of a whole community.

The sons of New Hampshire may rejoice that theirs was the first state to provide by law that towns may raise and spend money in support of libraries. This library looks to the town for its direction, use, and support. Hereafter every one in Warner will be subject to the test, What think you of the library? Do you use and support it? It may be appropriate to suggest another thought. Is not here the opportunity for preserving, in connection with your library, a collection of local relics? Such objects, associated with our ancestors or events of other days, speak of the past, and are naturally associated with books and history, so well called philosophy;—teaching by example, both shall speak from the book and illustrate to the eye.

St. Martin is said to have observed,—" We are climbing up this life as if on a ladder. In death this ladder is snatched from us, and we then stand in that region of life to which each had himself attained." Spurgeon calls idleness " the key to beggary;" so it may be the open door to degradation. A good book for every idle hour would save multitudes from falling, and make many an idler a doer of worthy deeds. In our upward climbing there may come to us, through the library, the great achievements of mankind and the voices of the great and good from every age and clime, uniting in bearing one message to every aspiring soul expressed in the single word " Excelsior," while the angel of approval offers to every attainment the garland of reward.

REMARKS OF S. C. PATTEE, ESQ.

MR. PRESIDENT, LADIES AND GENTLEMEN: It is with the greatest pleasure that I rise to express my heartfelt thanks to Mr. and Mrs. Pillsbury for the munificent gift they have this day so generously bestowed upon our people—a gift, I trust, that we shall appreciate more and more as time moves on, and we begin to see and taste its ripened fruit.

It is truly a beautiful gift. The building is beautiful because of its adaptedness to the purposes for which it was designed, and for its architecture, its exquisite finish, and the solid and imperishable materials of which it is constructed; but the most beautiful part is to be found within its alcoves and recesses. Books! books!—rich and rare, grave and gay, science and fiction, containing the thoughts, researches, biography, and travels of our best men and women. With this beautiful structure, and with its rich and numerous volumes within reach of all our citizens, it cannot but develop and fix a habit of reading among all classes that will make us wiser men and women.

In the declaration of purposes of the order of Patrons of Husbandry we find this phrase,—"to develop a higher manhood and womanhood among ourselves;" and when Warner Grange heard that Mr. Pillsbury had decided to present to the town of Warner a valuable library building, its members were enthusiastic, and arose with one accord and passed a vote of thanks to Mr. Pillsbury, and pledged themselves to perpetuate and maintain, by every word and deed and act, so valuable an institution in our midst; "for how," said they, "can we better fulfil our purpose of developing a better manhood and womanhood among ourselves than by reading good books?"

When Mr. Pillsbury resided in town I was a boy, at work on my father's farm; and I well remember that Mr. Pillsbury was always foremost in advocating and building up all institutions that were for the moral and social benefit of the people, especially in temperance matters. I never shall forget with what zeal he labored with me, to induce me to join the order of the Sons of Temperance. I consented, but had not the ready cash to pay my membership fees. Mr. Pillsbury generously put his hand in his pocket and advanced the money. That was a small matter, Mr. President, but little things have great endings sometimes. That little germ of generosity in Mr. Pillsbury has been growing all these years, until now the bud has burst open, and the marvellous beauty of his generosity and that of his beloved wife fills us with gratitude and pleasure. May its seeds be scattered broadcast over our town, and may you, Mr. and Mrs. Pillsbury, live long to see the harvest garnered in —a noble manhood and womanhood—from the valleys and the hills which you so much love.

ADDRESS OF PROF. C. J. EMERSON.

MR. PRESIDENT, LADIES AND GENTLEMEN: When God piled up the hills and scooped out the valleys of New Hampshire, he prepared a birthplace for virtue, patriotism, and all the characteristics of stalwart manhood. When he smoothed down the plains of the South and stretched out the prairies of the West, he prepared fitting fields for bold and energetic enterprise. The East has produced a host of men, eager and able to do; and the West has afforded ample opportunity for doing.

We are proud of our mountain state,—with her forests and her streams, her beautiful lakes and her rugged soil; but we are doubly proud of her men and women. Noble in purpose and grand in integrity, they have maintained the honor of their native state from the limits of the East to the farthest West. There is a wonderful amount of affection wrapped up in the hearts of her sons and daughters, who love to revisit the scenes of early years, where youth was in its bloom, and love and hope were strong and buoyant. To the generosity of such men we are indebted to-day for our beautiful library. It is a royal gift, worth far more than city bonds or deeds of real estate. Free to every citizen of the town, it is a treasury from which may be drawn infinite stores of benefit and happiness.

With the making and reading of books, civilization began. The Pentateuch of Moses and the poems of Homer and of Hesiod are the germs of that universal library that has raised the enlightened nations up from the darkness of barbarism.

In all countries and in all ages the prosperity and happiness of a people have been in direct proportion to their literary culture. Go into any town or city where education is general and books circulate freely, and you will find the people intelligent and orderly, the streets trim and well kept, the houses well painted, and the wife with a smile greeting her husband at the door.

He who has acquired a taste for good reading is a companion for kings and princes; yea, more, he is the intimate associate of the true heroes of all ages. At his will he enjoys the wit of Sheridan, the logic of Burke, and the wisdom of Franklin. Would he revel in tournaments where grace and beauty are the rewards of knightly deeds, then he reads the volumes of Scott; would he while away the restful hours of a summer's afternoon, then he takes from the shelves the poems of Longfellow, of Goldsmith, and of Burns; when the old warlike spirit stirs his blood, and the pulse beats hot with its quickened load, he reads the lives of Alexander, of Cæsar, and of Napoleon; when every mood would be gratified to which the mind is susceptible, the family gather around the table of a winter's evening, and read the works of Shakespeare and of Dickens.

He who reads not at all is one man; he who makes himself master of the thoughts and experiences of one good author is two men; he who understands the works of two great writers is three men, and so on. By this mode of enumeration, we hope in the near future the population of Warner will be one hundred thousand.

Believe me, sir, the people of Warner are deeply grateful for this princely gift. Like a beautiful river that flows between constantly receding banks till it is finally lost in the tides and swells of the ocean, so the influences from this library shall extend and progress through coming ages till they are embraced and enjoyed by countless generations.

REMARKS OF REV. A. E. HALL.

MR. CHAIRMAN, LADIES AND GENTLEMEN: I am sure we feel very much alike to-day. Truly, we are with one accord in one place. How delightful it all is! Something more than the touch that "makes the whole world kin" has thrilled our bosoms as we have listened to the words spoken by our benefactor, reminiscent of the far off years when he came with his loving bride to purchase citizenship in this goodly town; came to join hands and hearts, in noble endeavor to strengthen and perpetuate her institutions, with the venerable men and women, a few of whom remain to come here to-day to extend hands of welcome and loving greeting, and to renew the blessed fellowships of the other years. We have watched the play of emotions, too deep and eloquent to be uttered in words, which flitted from face to face all over this great audience of souls, as, with countenance lifted in light upon us, Mr. Pillsbury told how, away in his Western home, he took counsel with his dear wife how they might adequately express their gratitude to God for the good prosperity vouchsafed them, and the affection which lingered in their hearts for the scenes and associations of their early years; and how together they projected and fashioned the idea which shall be a legacy of good to the inhabitants of this town forever, to commemorate which we are met here on this happy occasion. We have heard the fitting words of praise uttered in prose and in verse by cultured lips and from overflowing hearts in honor of all who have lent aid to this splendid beneficence, and our hearts have responded to every syllable with quickened pulse. The spirits within us have had their exhilaration and glow softened and melodized by the delicious music, which, mingling with the incense of grateful hearts, has risen up before this altar, pervading this vast assembly with its sweet vitality. And now it would seem that only one thing further is needed to make this hour's festivities complete,—to associate this splendid beneficence with the dear Father above, from whom cometh every perfect gift.

> "Praise God from whom all blessings flow;
> Praise Him, all creatures here below;
> Praise Him above, ye heavenly host;
> Praise Father, Son, and Holy Ghost!"

REV. ROBERT BENNETT.

Mr. Bennett's speech was unreportable. He alluded to the occasion when the chairman called him to the platform at the town-meeting, which was crowded with voters, many of whom were doubtful whether the terms of Mr. Pillsbury's gift would be accepted by the town. He recalled the words of the chairman, "Get to the front," and he replied that he would do so; and after his speech the overwhelming vote in the affirmative, without a solitary No, attested that he did.

He made a congratulatory comparison between

Mr. Pillsbury and himself, remarking the pleasing coincidence that they were both Suttonians,—Mr. Pillsbury being a Sutton, N. H., boy, and he a boy of the older Sutton, England.

In conclusion, he paid a glowing tribute to the sons and citizens of Warner whom the orator and poet had so justly praised, adding that while the glorious deeds of the men and women of the past generations were worthy of all praise, her coming sons and daughters would, like stars and suns, illumine her future destiny with a greater splendor, and her records with an ever increasing fame; and it was his heartfelt pride to stand in the grand ancestral line as a father of one of Warner's sons!

REMARKS OF GILMAN C. GEORGE, ESQ.

Mr. Chairman and Fellow-Citizens: This is preëminently a red-letter day for Warner, a day long to be remembered. We have been more highly favored than most other towns, in many respects. We enjoy more and better railroad facilities than almost any other town through which the road is constructed. We have our agricultural fair, where the husbandmen display the products of our fertile soil, the fine herds of cattle which graze and fatten upon our rugged hills and in our pleasant valleys, the blooded horses which some of our citizens are noted for raising, and where are shown the various kinds of handiwork which our matrons are so justly celebrated for producing. We have our mountain road, which affords the most enchanting view from the summit of Mt. Kearsarge. We have a Masonic Lodge, an Odd Fellows Lodge, and a Grange,—all of which are well patronized and in prosperous condition. We also have the Simonds Free High School, the doors of which are open for the admission of all the young people of the town of requisite age and requirements, and where they may prepare themselves for almost any position, either in public or in private life. And last, though by no means least, through the munificent generosity of a former resident, seconded by one of our own citizens in the donation of grounds for the site, we have a Free Public Library, to the rich and varied literature of which all the citizens of the town will have free and equal access, and from whose well filled shelves they can select such books as may be suited to their individual tastes. We congratulate the donors on being in circumstances to make such a liberal donation; and we may well congratulate ourselves on being the recipients of such bounty.

God bless the donors! Long may they live; and may their shadows never be less!

REMARKS OF DR. J. R. COGSWELL.

MR. PRESIDENT, LADIES AND GENTLEMEN: It will be unnecessary for me to go upon the platform, as I have no set speech prepared for this occasion.

I was early consulted as to the advisability of a free library for Warner, and gave my hearty approval of the scheme. I have ever said and done what I could to induce the people to accept and appreciate this noble gift of Mr. Pillsbury's, the magnitude of which can scarcely be estimated at this time. Our people are usually alive to their best interests; and it gave me much pleasure to have them vote unanimously to accept the generous gift, and to tax themselves to support it. I was proud then to be a citizen of Warner, and am still more proud to-day, after listening to these dedicatory exercises; proud, that with almost entirely home talent we have made this occasion one long to be remembered. I may be pardoned for saying that not every town, even in New Hampshire, can boast of such talent and culture as are necessary to bring forth such literary productions as we have listened to here to-day.

It gives me great pleasure to see so many people here to assist in these exercises, and especially to see these aged men and women, who for nearly fourscore years have resided in our town, and who have ever, as now, been found on the side of progress and improvement.

And now, fellow-citizens, that we have a free library building—a gem of art—well built and well-nigh imperishable, and also thousands of volumes of well selected books, what shall we do with them? We can make the most of these useful gifts only by cultivating a taste for reading, and for reading the best books, so that we may derive both pleasure and profit. Let us read to improve both mind and heart, and not forget to lay in such knowledge as will help us to perfect ourselves physically. Let us all be very thankful for these our great opportunities.

Our town has great natural advantages, and we ought to see to it that people from far and near shall be invited to view our beautiful green valleys and high hills and grand old mountains, so that many more may come to dwell with us, at least during the pleasant, health-giving months of the summer and autumn. There is no better town in "The Switzerland of America" for the sojourn of summer tourists than Warner. Here are many things which go to make life pleasant—a flourishing business town, with happy homes, intelligent people, fine schools, a free high school, and last, but not least, a free library. Let us all appreciate these our great and enduring privileges.

REMARKS OF DR. J. M. RIX.

MR. PRESIDENT, LADIES AND GENTLEMEN: It is with a good deal of diffidence that I rise on this occasion, in response to the invitation of the president of the day, to attempt to make any remarks, and especially to so large and intelligent an audience as I see here to-day; and more especially since those who have preceded me have been preparing for this occasion, and have addressed you in such felicitous, eloquent, and appropriate language. While I do not propose to attempt to make any extended remarks at this late hour, the thought comes into my mind that I may stand here as an humble representative of a class of citizens, scattered all over our broad land, whose deeds of valor have made this occasion possible, and who, with those who fell when the chain of these United States was broken by the boom of the first cannon at Sumter, hastened, at the call of our great captain, Lincoln, to help weld the chain anew in the best blood of our beloved land,—so that the glory of a united, redeemed, and prosperous country shines more clearly to-day than ever before. I am reminded of these things by the fact that members of Robert Campbell Post, G. A. R., have just returned from paying the last tribute of esteem and respect to a deceased comrade, a gallant soldier in the late Rebellion, and an upright and honored citizen, one who in the late Civil War achieved a noble record. Comrade Leonidas Harriman, whose remains we have laid to rest to-day in the quiet of Pine Grove cemetery, was respected and beloved by every member of the post to which he belonged; and he will be sadly missed by his sorrowing friends and comrades from the roll-call of domestic associations and from the Grand Army of the Republic. Comrade Harriman did his duty grandly as a soldier, and then came back to receive the plaudits and gratitude of a generous people. Without the patriotic services of such as he, carried to a successful termination, would such occasions as this have been realized, with a country torn asunder by factions and clans, secession following secession, until the proud republic of the Western Hemisphere had disappeared from among the nations of the earth? Then should we have had need of so princely a gift as this, which we receive and so highly cherish to-day? Should we have had a government to guarantee and establish a title to the spot of this green earth which has been so generously given, and on which has been erected this beautiful structure, and to-day dedicated to the uplifting, educating, and advancement of this people for all future time?

And I will only say further, that my feelings are entirely in harmony with the spirit that pervades all present, and that has brought us together to-day; and to all that has been said here, to all the sentiments expressed in prose or poesy, I can heartily say, Amen.

REMARKS OF FRANK P. HARRIMAN, ESQ., OF BOSTON.

Mr. President, Ladies and Gentlemen: I did not anticipate taking part in these exercises until this moment. Called here on a sad mission to my native town, to bury another dear brother, and comrade as well, I am on this account permitted to be with you. As most of you are aware, I belong to what was once a very large family, most of whom now, and in a short time all of whom will, sleep beneath Warner's soil. To be born and buried here is our lot.

We have been treated this afternoon to sweet music, inspiring poetry, oratory, and eloquence. The exercises have been of a high order, of which all may well feel both pleased and proud. They have, however, been pretty long, and it is getting late, and I must not detain you:—but I am reminded of a kissing party I attended in good old Warner when I was a boy. We had such a good time we did not want to go home, so we stayed till three o'clock in the morning. The householder, who took no part in the fun, said, after we were gone,

"They had a good party, but if they had stayed an hour longer they would have ruined the whole business."

But I am deeply interested in all that pertains to the welfare of my dear old native town, though it has not been my home for nearly twenty-five years. I am heartily glad you have this library. It is fortunate that the town has such a benefactor as my old friend Mr. Pillsbury, whom I remember as a leading citizen of the town when I was a boy. I remember, too, the first libraries in town, which my father and some of the ladies and gentlemen present helped to establish. I remember my first book taken from one of these libraries, The Swiss Family Robinson, and this was in the vicinity of forty-five years ago; and that same book is now in the high-school library, if it has been preserved. When these first small libraries were established in Warner, we could not foresee, in the dim perspective, one of our number, out of the kindness of his heart and from the abundance of a well merited prosperity, coming back from the distant West to a ten years' adopted home to found such an institution as this—such a well ordered building of architectural beauty, together with such a large and valuable collection of books.

This gift, friends, is a blessing both to the giver and to the receiver. Its influence cannot be measured. The middle-aged, and the old, even, will take great satisfaction in it. The young, not only of to-day, but of all time, will be influenced by it, and they will carry that influence out into the world.

The anticipations of those who have been looking and hoping for an institution of this kind are now more than realized, and in joining hands to sustain it you are one and all making the wheel of progress whirl, which you, as citizens of America, remember, are bound by birth to do.

At the conclusion of F. P. Harriman's remarks, ex-Governor Ordway stepped to the front of the platform and said that Chairman Fred Bean, and his associates composing the board of selectmen, had honored themselves and delighted the whole people of the town by specially inviting large numbers of the fathers and mothers of the town, who had reached from three to four score years, to honorary seats upon the platform, where they could in comparative ease and comfort listen to these dedicatory exercises and enjoy the rich musical treat with which Blaisdell's orchestra was inspiring the whole audience. He said he now, by permission of the chairman, took great pleasure in introducing the oldest citizen of the town, perhaps the oldest merchant in Merrimack county, under whose tutelage he himself had learned the a b c's of business, Mr. Robert Thompson, who, although fast nearing his eighty-ninth year, was as straight as an arrow, and who, as the Dean of all the Warner libraries, would give his extended knowledge of them and of many of the early settlers and leading families of the town.

Mr. Thompson, whose hearing has been somewhat impaired by the weight of years, stepped briskly to the front of the platform, and without notes or preparation spoke substantially as follows:

REMARKS OF ROBERT THOMPSON, ESQ.

MR. PRESIDENT, LADIES AND GENTLEMEN: I have made no preparation for speaking here to-day, nor had I any expectation of doing so. I have listened to all who have spoken with great pleasure; but you may think it strange when I say I have not heard one word that was said, but I tried to use my eyes.

Perhaps there is no other person present who remembers the first Warner library, or that there was one in early times. I have been a resident of this town for sixty-six years, and in all that time have never been absent ten consecutive days. I came here a boy, and grew to know the people well. I was an orphan boy, and the old people liked me, or at least I liked them, and they were like fathers and mothers to me. My interests have been here, and to-day I love the town as I do my life.

When I came here sixty-six years ago, the town had been settled about a hundred years, and what do you think I found? I found a very intelligent set of men and women, who were the first settlers and proprietors; I rejoice to say I have seen and conversed with some of them. There were Ensign Currier, Jacob Collins, and Zebulon Davis; and of the next generation, General Aquila Davis, and Wells Davis, his brother, and Joseph, Richard, and Simeon Bartlett, and Benjamin Evans. They hewed out the paths from one home to another, built the roads and the bridges, started schools and churches. And what else did I find? The " Warner Town Library," which the early inhabitants had established; and it was read, too, by most of the inhabitants. In quite early times the Congregationalists started a Sabbath-school, and soon had a library, but it was not the Warner library; then the Baptists, in 1834, built a church and had a Sabbath-school library, but that was not the Warner library. The town, as a town, would not go to either for books. Then there was a five-dollar library, which some objected to on account of its cost; so a two-dollar one was subscribed to, and perhaps one or two others. The Thompson library, called the Kearsarge circulating library, of a few hundred volumes, had a good circulation and was well read. These all flourished for a while, and then went out. But none of these were the Warner library. Then came the high-school library,—small at first; but a few years ago, through the efforts of the librarian, Miss Mary B. Harris, by writing to old residents and soliciting for it, it began to increase. Money or books were contributed, until the number of volumes has increased to over eleven hundred. But the one I found here sixty-six years ago was called the "Warner Town Library." I have seen the books, and have two or three in my possession now. Perhaps I am talking too long, and you are not interested; but I tell you this that you may know, as a matter of history, that there was once before a town library, and that this, which my life-long friend, George A. Pillsbury, has so generously given to us, our children, and our children's children, is once more a "Warner Town Library."

LETTER FROM COL. JOHN B. CLARKE.

WARNER, N. H., September 29, 1891.

To Frederick Myron Colby, Secretary Trustees of Pillsbury Free Library:

I have received your invitation, on behalf of the trustees of the Pillsbury Free Library, to make a brief speech at the dedication of the library on the 2d prox. As business calls me away this week, and I may not be able to return in season for the dedication exercises, I take this method to express my high appreciation of the generous beneficence of George A. Pillsbury, and to congratulate the inhabitants of Warner upon a gift so fraught with blessings to the people of this beautiful town for all coming time.

Until the present season, my knowledge of Warner was limited pretty much to an acquaintance with some of her most prominent sons (and one or two of her daughters). The late Governor E. A. Straw, so many years the foremost man in our own city, and one of the ablest men in many respects this state has produced, had his birthplace here, and when, a few weeks since, I passed the house where he was born, on Tory hill, I felt like lifting my hat as a mark of respect to his memory. The late Governor Harriman, whose eloquent voice was known all over the land, was proud of his native town, and wrote her history with loving pen.

And yet another governor was born in Warner, and still goes in and out among you, and, by his generous gift of the land upon which your beautiful library building stands, ex-Governor N. G.

Ordway shares with Mr. Pillsbury in this benefaction to his native town. Any town might be proud to number among its sons three such men as the governors named; yet there are many other sons and daughters of Warner, living and dead, who have achieved distinction in literary, professional, and political walks; but I will not attempt to enumerate them here.

If Warner has reason to be proud of her own sons and daughters, may she not also plume herself upon those who are here only by adoption? Surely at this time every citizen feels both pride in and affection for the man who in so munificent a manner testifies the love he bears to the place where he spent the first years of his struggling young manhood, getting the experience so helpful to him in laying the foundations of the magnificent fortune he has built up in the far West, and which he is so nobly, so wisely, devoting to public benefactions,— a library here, a monument there, a hospital elsewhere, and so on,—doing good with his fortune while he lives, and not, as so many wealthy men have done, keeping it for greedy heirs to quarrel over after he has gone.

And the orator who has been chosen to address you, our senator, William E. Chandler, who now for many years has made Warner his summer home, and who loves it, as he tells me, more and more the longer he stays, may well be reckoned as one of Warner's own distinguished citizens.

No one, it seems to me, who has any appreciation of the beauties of nature can fail to be charmed with the scenery of Warner. With a somewhat extended acquaintance with the most picturesque portions of our state, I do not recall any town which affords so many charming drives and so many superb landscape views as I have found during my sojourn in Warner the present season.

But it is not your scenery alone which makes Warner a desirable place of residence. I find here many excellent farms and superb pastures, and some very progressive farmers. There are good horses and cattle and sheep. There is a thriving manufactory, which gives employment to numerous people and a business impetus to the town. There are live, active merchants to supply your wants, and you need not go out of town for an orator, a poet, a lawyer, a doctor, or a story-writer, even if you aim pretty high. You have a flourishing grange, which is doing much to educate the people; and a good local newspaper whereby the needs and the doings of the town may be made known. You have your excellent free high school, where your children may receive a good education. Now the Pillsbury Free Library adds the crowning blessing; and with all these advantages Warner should be not only a good place to be born in, but to live in, to stay in, and to return to if one has strayed away—I will not say, to die in, because I have not yet thought of any good place in which to die. It now only needs the united, hearty efforts of the citizens of the town to make Warner a more prosperous and thriving and altogether delightful place than it has ever been.

Very respectfully yours,
JOHN B. CLARKE.

The exercises closed with a benediction by Rev. Robert Bennett.

EVENING RECEPTION.

The people of Warner, feeling that some mark of respect should be shown to their benefactors, arranged for a reception to Mr. and Mrs. Pillsbury at the town hall in the evening, where every citizen might have an opportunity to greet them.

The reception, like the afternoon exercises, was a pronounced success. The committee on decoration had exercised taste and skill worthy of experts, and the refreshment table was a thing of beauty. The reception committee, who accompanied Mr. and Mrs. Pillsbury to the stage, where the vast crowd which filled every part of the standing-room in the hall passed along to take them by the hand, were Honorable and Mrs. N. G. Ordway, Colonel and Mrs. John B. Clarke, Mr. and Mrs. A. P. Davis, Mr. and Mrs. A. C. Carroll, Dr. and Mrs. J. R. Cogswell, Mr. and Mrs. H. C. Davis, Dr. and Mrs. J. M. Rix, Mr. and Mrs. F. M. Colby, Mr. and Mrs. B. F. Heath, Mr. and Mrs. F. G. Wilkins. Fred Bean, chairman of the board of selectmen, was chairman of the evening. Blaisdell's orchestra furnished music; and the two hours spent here rounded out a day replete with happiness to all who participated.

MARGARET PILLSBURY GENERAL HOSPITAL.

CONCORD, NEW HAMPSHIRE.

THE MARGARET PILLSBURY GENERAL HOSPITAL.

The Margaret Pillsbury General Hospital occupies a pleasant site on Turnpike street, overlooking the Merrimack valley, and commanding an extensive view of the hills and forest upon the east side of the river. It is in full view from the cars of all passenger trains entering or departing from the city on the south, and attracts attention by its imposing and substantial appearance. It is one hundred twenty-four feet long, and seventy-five feet in width at the two ends, which project a few feet beyond the central part of the building. Its height is forty-five feet—two stories and a basement, slated roof, with ventilating cupola. The basement is of Concord granite, the walls of pressed brick with granite and terra-cotta trimmings, and the cornices and water-conduits are of copper. The main entrance is at the north-east corner of the building, protected by an ample porte-cochère. At the north end is another entrance, beneath a porch upheld by terra-cotta pillars, and on each side of it the walls are semi-circular, presenting a handsome appearance when approached from the city. The central part of the east front bears in raised granite letters the words,

MARGARET PILLSBURY GENERAL HOSPITAL

At the main entrance is an open vestibule with tiled floor, and upon the left wall is a tablet which bears this inscription:

<blockquote>
ERECTED BY
GEORGE ALFRED PILLSBURY.
IN HONOR OF HIS WIFE
MARGARET SPRAGUE PILLSBURY.
ON THE FIFTIETH ANNIVERSARY
OF THEIR MARRIAGE.
1891
</blockquote>

The two entrances open into a large hall, from which access is easy to the executive departments of the hospital and to the waiting- and operating-rooms. At the right of the main entrance is the trustees' room, and back of this and connecting with it is the physicians' consulting-room. On the left of the main entrance is the waiting-room for visitors, separated from the hall by a screen of oak, surmounted with grill work. The main staircase springs from the hall on the west of the visitors' room. On the west of the north entrance is the large operating-room, admirably lighted by large windows on the north, with tiled floor, and furnished with all necessary conveniences. A corridor west from the hall leads to the commodious and well appointed kitchen and pantry, both finished in oak.

From the kitchen a dumb-waiter runs to the serving-room on the second floor.

Leading south from the hall is a wide corridor, on either side of which are matron's dining-room, sewing-room, dispensary, linen- and clothes-rooms, serving-room, bath-rooms, and water-closets, several private wards, and at the extreme south end, on either side, are two general wards, with capacity for eight and five beds respectively. In each of these wards is an open fire-place of brick with oak mantel and mirror, and above each bed is suspended an electric button to summon nurses when the patient requires attention.

The second floor is reached by the main staircase from the hall, and by a staircase midway of the west side of the lower corridor. At the north end are rooms for the matron and nurses, with electric-bell and speaking-tube connection to all parts of the building. A corridor, with rooms and wards similar to those on the lower floor, extends to the south end of the building, and opens upon a spacious and sunny balcony for the use of convalescent patients. In the north-west corner of the second floor, cut off from the rest of the building and reached by a separate staircase connecting with the rear entrance of the hospital, is the isolated ward for contagious diseases. In the attic are five comfortable rooms for the help, finished in the centre of the building, and there is abundant room in the ends of the building on this floor for additional rooms, should occasion require them.

The basement, which extends under the entire structure, contains the hot-water heating apparatus and fresh-air pipes, and storage-rooms for kitchen, table, and dietary supplies. The heating is controlled by an automatic electric mechanism, which raises or lowers the temperature in every room, when it varies slightly from the required degree to which the thermometer is set. Each room has a register and ventilator, the latter connected by galvanized iron pipes with the central ventilating shaft running from the basement. The corridors and halls are heated by numerous radiators. The entire building is wired for electric lights and piped for gas lights. The finish (doors, casings, and mouldings) is of quartered oak; the floors are of birch and marble, deadened with mineral wool; and the adamant walls are finished in two colors. The heating apparatus is located in the north end of the basement, far away from the wards; and the laundry is a one-story structure on the west of the north end, and is easily accessible from the basement.

The hospital has accommodations for fifty patients, and is an elegant and substantial structure, with the most approved appointments suggested by medical and surgical experts.

DEDICATORY EXERCISES.

The hospital was dedicated on Monday afternoon, October 5, 1891, the exercises being held in the south end of the corridor on the lower floor, and the auditors occupying the general wards and the corridor, completely filling them. Blaisdell's orchestra played several selections while the audience were gathering, and at three o'clock the exercises opened with singing by the Crescent Quartette, after which Hon. Samuel C. Eastman, president of the Hospital Association, presented Hon. George A. Pillsbury, as the first speaker, in these words:

LADIES AND GENTLEMEN: We are assembled to receive the gift of this structure, so admirably fitted for the purposes for which it is designed, and to dedicate it to the relief of the suffering and afflicted. I have the honor to present to you the donor, Hon. George Alfred Pillsbury, formerly of this city, but now of Minneapolis, Minnesota.

Mr. Pillsbury said,—

MR. CHAIRMAN OF THE BOARD OF TRUSTEES OF THE MARGARET PILLSBURY GENERAL HOSPITAL:—SIR: On the 1st day of March, 1852, I became a resident of the city of Concord, and remained here for about twenty-six years, until the 20th day of March, 1878. During my residence here I became very much attached to its people, and took a lively interest in whatever I thought would promote its advantage. I have abundant reason to love and respect the people of this city, for during my residence here every honor within their gift was conferred upon me. Since I left Concord, I have been somewhat successful so far as this world's goods are concerned. I have been pleasantly situated in the beautiful city of Minneapolis, in the far-off state of Minnesota. I have, however, never forgotten my native state nor the beautiful city of

Concord. I love to visit New Hampshire, and look upon her hills and mountains and admire her beautiful scenery. I love also to visit the city of Concord. I have been in every state of the Union, and in all of its territories except three. I have also visited at least thirteen foreign countries; and I can truthfully say, that if I were to change my present place of residence, I know of no city that I should prefer, all things considered, to this city of Concord.

For a year or two I have thought that I should like to do something that would be acceptable to the people of your city, and that would be of a lasting benefit to all of its people. I have for many years been of the opinion that it was the duty of every one, as far as possible, to administer upon his own estate. We have had frequent examples where the ablest of lawyers have failed to draw a will that would be sustained by the courts. I have also noticed, during my somewhat prolonged life, that property left to children has proved, I think in a majority of cases, a curse rather than a blessing, especially where such children are possessed of strong bodies and a good education;—of course the facts would be different in cases of invalids.

Several objects presented themselves to my mind, all of them good in themselves. Learning that your city was in need of a better hospital building, and after talking the matter over with my wife, with whom I had spent about fifty years of married life, we came to the conclusion that perhaps we could not do a better thing than to supply this need; and so, after correspondence and consultation with your board of trustees, plans were made, submitted to them, and adopted, and the building was commenced.

Ground was broken in September, 1890, and we are here to-day to turn over to your organization this completed building, together with a deed of the ground upon which it stands. We wish it to be distinctly understood that it is designed as a gift to the people of Concord. It is hoped that your organization will so conduct its affairs that its benefits shall be shared first by your own citizens, and then by others, as its means will afford. Let it be an institution where the sick and unfortunate of all classes can be cared for, and restored to health, if possible, and be made comfortable during their stay here.

This building has cost much more than I expected at the start. I have endeavored to make a substantial, durable, and convenient building for the purpose for which it was designed.

The plans were prepared by Mr. Warren B. Dunnell, of Minneapolis, Minnesota, who has had large experience in making plans for buildings of similar purpose. The plans were submitted to your board of trustees, and any suggestions made have been adopted. The intention has been to make it as perfect in all respects as any in the country for one of its size. How well I have succeeded you can judge for yourselves. The name given to this building was suggested by me, and was adopted by your board. This I intended as a token of love and esteem to the partner of my life, who has for more than fifty years been a true and faithful companion, and has ever shared with me the trials, perplexities, and anxieties, as well as the pleasures, of these fifty years. She has cordially united with me in the erection of this building. We hope and expect, under the management of your board of trustees and your successors in office, that, as a result of the erection of this hospital building, the sick, the maimed, and all classes of the unfortunate will receive the best possible care and treatment. I believe that many persons die for the want of proper treatment. The poor are in many instances unable to provide proper medical aid and nursing, and as a result suffer a lingering, painful death; others, more able, are ignorant as to proper care, and death comes to their beloved ones from no known fault of theirs. I am extremely well pleased to know that you have on your board so many cultivated and Christian women; I hope this will ever be the case. I believe they can do more, in many cases that will be treated here, than those of the other sex. I think you have been extremely fortunate in having associated with you ladies who have been willing and ready, as Christians, to devote so much of their time and attention to the inmates of your hospital.

I think the people of Concord owe a debt of gratitude to the physicians who have, without pay, rendered so much valuable service to the interests of the unfortunate who have been brought here. What better test of a true, enlightened Christian manhood and womanhood can be made than to take care of the unfortunate, who are unable to take care of themselves in the hour of their adversity!

The foundation for this building was laid by Messrs. Brown & Abbott, of Concord. The building was built by Mr. E. B. Hutchinson, also of Concord. The heating apparatus has been put in by A. A. Pond, of Minneapolis; the plumbing, by Messrs. Lee Brothers, of Concord; the Johnson Heat and Regulating apparatus, by the Johnson Electric Service Company, of Milwaukee; the speaking tubes and electric bells, by the Manchester Heating and Lighting Company. Mr. Giles Wheeler has superintended the construction of the building in all its parts, and I believe each and all have performed their duties faithfully and well. The gas fixtures were contracted for with C. H. McKenney & Co., of Boston, through Lee Brothers, of this city; but as they failed to put them in by September 29th last, as by agreement, the contract has been annulled, and other parties will be employed for that purpose. And now allow myself and wife to present to you a deed of the land upon which this building stands, also the keys to the building itself.

In accepting the gift from Mr. Pillsbury, in behalf of the hospital, Mr. Eastman said,—

In behalf of the trustees of the Margaret Pillsbury General Hospital, I accept this noble and generous gift which you have been pleased to bestow upon the city of Concord. For, sir, while your gift is to the Margaret Pillsbury General Hospital in name, we and our citizens all well understand that it is to the fact that the Association represents the people of the city which was so long your home, that we are indebted for the honor of being selected as the almoner of your bounty. I cannot find words to express adequately the deep sense of gratitude with which this gift is received by the citizens of Concord. They well remember the spirit of public enterprise which was so marked a characteristic of all that you did when you lived among us, and recognize in this act only its more perfect development. As trustees, we join most heartily and specially in the thanks we now offer you, and assure you that as time goes on our feelings of gratitude and respect will be continually renewed and strengthened by the ever recurring realization of the benefits you have conferred upon us.

Nor, sir, will the grateful recognition of your benefaction be confined to us who are here present and our successors. While kings and emperors have deemed triumphal arches and statues the most fitting memorials of their great deeds, you, with what we must be allowed to commend as the nobler Christian course, have seen fit to select, as a memorial of the good-will which you and your esteemed wife cherish towards the suffering and the afflicted, that which for generations yet to come will minister to the sick, and alleviate in some degree the ills to which all are subject. As the thousands of patients within these walls shall call to mind to whom they are indebted for the kindly shelter which they have found in their hour of need, they will hold your memory dear, and thank God for the inspiration given you to execute this noble charity.

You have given us, sir, the best hospital building of its size to be found in the New England states. Its fitness for the work for which it is designed, the thoroughness of its construction, the beauty of its finish, the ingenuity of its many devices, its complete ventilation, the convenience of its arrangement for the saving of labor of nurses and attendants, all testify to the skill of the architect, to the care and solicitude of the mind which provided for all, and to the loving-kindness of the heart which dictated the plan to be pursued. Where every detail has been made as perfect as modern science and human wisdom could devise, it was impossible not to produce the best. We feel that we have the right to be proud of our city, proud of our hospital, and, above all, proud that a a man and a woman of such noble aims have deemed us worthy of their friendship and esteem.

As we are now entering a larger sphere of usefulness, it seems proper to glance briefly at the history and development of the existing organization.

No doubt the idea and need of a hospital for the care of the sick and injured had occurred to the minds of many, and had even been suggested in public, before the plan of the Hospital Association was matured. The first action, however, which had a visible and tangible result was due to the energy and enthusiasm of Dr. Shadrach C. Morrill. He was the first to take the matter in hand in a practical form. With that earnest zeal which characterizes all his acts when his conviction is awakened, he began by soliciting contributions from his friends. In fact, nearly all the money that was raised for the first year, and a very large part of the second year's subscriptions, came from his exertions. Having received the promise of a considerable sum of money, he invited the coöperation of his brother physicians and others, and the Hospital Association of Concord was legally organized as a corporation on the evening of July 3, 1884.

About three months were consumed in finding a suitable location and house, in furnishing it, and in procuring a matron. A trained nurse was considered to be beyond the means of the Association at that time. The physicians of Concord readily and cheerfully gave their services without remuneration, and the various religious associations, as well as some individuals, assumed then and subsequently the furnishing of rooms.

Seven years ago this very month the hospital received its first patient in the building which has ever since been occupied for the same purpose. At the time of the annual meeting, in January following, when the first annual report was made, nine patients had been received. Up to the present time nearly seven hundred different patients have been admitted to the hospital. When we advert to the fact that in almost all these cases resort was had to the hospital because good care and nursing could not be had elsewhere, we see that the institution has had a very important mission to perform in our community. From the fact that it has been almost wholly supported by contributions from our own citizens, as well as from the lack of room, its good work has thus far been chiefly confined to our own territorial limits. With the increased accommodations which will now be afforded, and with the additional aid which we have no doubt will be forthcoming, its means of alleviating suffering will, we trust, be more largely extended in the future.

The contributions for the first year were $3,090, and the total amount contributed for the current expenses, and repairs and alterations, down to the end of 1890, is $18,140. The amount received from patients during the same period is $18,598, and from the city of Concord, for free beds, $5,700.

The permanent funds, on the first of January last, also gifts from citizens, amounted to $10,760, in which $2,120 interest had been received, and used for current expenses.

Our present hospital has cost, as nearly as I can estimate it, $12,000, of which $7,000 has been paid by voluntary contributions, the remaining $5,000 being a debt to be liquidated when the building and land are disposed of.

Three free beds have been founded, by the gift to the permanent funds of $5,000 in each case.

Rev. James Henry Eames, D. D., a native of Massachusetts and a graduate of Brown University, was for many years the loved and honored rector of St. Paul's church in this city. The present prosperity of the parish, as well as the building of the church, is almost wholly due to his skill as an organizer and to his deserved popularity as a minister. He was esteemed, honored, and respected, not only by his own congregation, but by all classes of our community, and his death was universally deplored.

Mrs. Jane Anthony Eames has given the first foundation in memory of her husband, the nomination of the beneficiaries being entrusted to St. Paul's church.

Benjamin F. Caldwell, one of our prominent citizens, was for a long time one of our leading manufacturers. He was the architect of his own fortune, a man of strong will and vigorous mind. The second foundation for a free bed was provided for by him in his will, and bears his name.

Mr. Joseph C. Hill was a native of Concord, and by his will gave the third foundation. His short life was full of promise, had it not been that his future was early clouded by ill health. He was a very great sufferer, especially during the last year of his life, from a painful disease superinduced by an accidental fall while yet a child. He bore his sufferings with an exceptional fortitude and cheerfulness, and his early death is lamented by a large circle of friends. The foundation is to bear his name.

The permanent funds to-day amount to $21,873.65, $15,000 of which is for the free beds; and the remainder consists of bequests or gifts in memory of Sargent C. Whitcher, Lyman Merrill, Calvin Howe, Reuben Lake, Francis A. Fisk, Mrs. Mary B. Coit, all of this city, and Mrs. Lizzie White Newhall, of Lynn, Mass., and Mary P. Ford, of Meredith, N. H., and of gifts by Mrs. Mary A. Stearns and Mrs. Mary C. H. Seavey, of Concord.

Other liberal and generous donors there are, who have contributed from year to year to the current expenses of the institution, whose names are recorded in the annual reports, and whom I wish we had time to mention. Besides gifts of money and of valuable and useful articles, the hospital has been largely aided by persons who have given their labor and time in a way which money could not buy. The ladies on the board of trustees, both those now members and those who for various reasons have found it necessary to resign, have rendered aid in the care of the hospital and the management of its domestic economy which has been invaluable, and without which the hospital would have fallen far short of success.

The Hon. Oliver Pillsbury was the first president of the Hospital Association. He was a man of culture and refinement. He devoted a great deal of time to the interests of the hospital, visiting it often, and laboring zealously in its behalf elsewhere. He demonstrated his lasting interest by making the Hospital Association his residuary legatee, from which bequest the permanent funds will eventually receive a large and important addition. The Association owes a debt to him which can never be repaid, for his faithful services in the early and formative days of its history.

The city of Concord, as a municipality, has also been a generous contributor. In 1886, $900 was voted for free beds, and every year since then we have been given $1,200 for the same purpose. The city has also procured a much needed ambulance for the conveyance of the sick and wounded. The presence here of his honor the mayor, who will address you upon the interest felt by the city in this cause, and of the members of the city council, shows that the hospital is, and will ever be, regarded as one of the institutions of the city entitled to confidence and support.

As a token of their appreciation of the generosity of Mr. Pillsbury, the trustees voted to change the name of the corporation to the Margaret Pillsbury General Hospital, and their action was ratified by a special act of the legislature of 1891. And to-day the Margaret Pillsbury General Hospital finds its capacities for good work enlarged. From the small and humble beginning in 1884, with four wards and seven beds, we find ourselves to-day equipped with this capacious building, with room for fifty beds, and all the convenient appliances and apparatus that such a building demands. From a local village institution we have developed into a general hospital, offering its resources and its benefits to a constantly enlarging circle of beneficiaries and patrons.

In this condition the trustees rightly feel that new responsibilities are thrust upon them. The old motto of the nobility, freely translated, inculcates upon the possessors of inherited rank the truth that a long line of noble ancestors imposes upon their descendants the obligation of living up to the standard that has been handed down to them, and transmitting it, in their turn, in due time, pure and unsullied, to the next generation. In somewhat the same spirit, the trustees to-day feel that by the generous benefactions that have been bestowed upon the organization, they and the whole community are under obligations to make redoubled efforts, not only for the physical, but for the spiritual and mental, welfare of those by whom we are surrounded, finding our compensation

> "In the soothing thoughts that spring
> Out of human suffering."

These new responsibilities are not, however, placed solely upon the trustees. While they are more directly chargeable for the proper administration of affairs, they cannot achieve a success, unless, like Moses, their hands are supported. They must continue to appeal with renewed solicitude to the good-will and aid of those who have so freely responded in the past, and beg them one and all to remember that the calls are constant, and that they must not weary in well-doing.

I hope that I do not need to assure you, sir, that, realizing these responsibilities, we receive this gift with the firm determination to execute the plan which has been formed in the most liberal and beneficent manner; nor to promise you, as I now do, not only in behalf of the trustees, but of the people of Concord, to whom you have given this memorial, that it shall always be sacredly devoted to the relief of suffering humanity. Have no fear that we shall fail, or even falter, in doing our part.

We are here not only to receive this the finest gift ever made to the people of Concord, but we to-day dedicate it with becoming ceremonies to the holy purposes for which it is designed. In doing this, we must not forget that while constructed for a noble and philanthropic use, it is also a memorial of the tender love cherished by an affectionate husband for a devoted wife, and to commemorate the fiftieth anniversary of their marriage. Fifty years of harmonious and loving union! How many memories of early struggles and trials in which each strengthened and supported the failing courage of the other! How many happy days when these trials were passed, and, as the years glided by, constant advances were made in the honor and esteem of their fellow-men, and more than all, in the satisfaction arising from the consciousness of duty performed and kindly aid extended to the less fortunate!

We celebrate a "golden wedding" made glorious by generous deeds and noble acts, and we dedicate a memorial unconsciously reared to the holy and endearing love of the family relation, the most sacred of human ties.

And now, sir, allow me, in behalf of all present, to offer to you, Mr. Pillsbury, and to you, Mrs. Pillsbury, our hearty congratulations on your attaining what is not granted to the many, and to express the hope that many other anniversaries, all unclouded by any sorrow, are yet in store for you.

Mr. Eastman then said,—

Without a medical staff there could be no hospital. Our medical staff, with unstinted zeal, have furnished the best services that science can supply, in season and out of season, without money and without price. As much a part of the organization as the trustees, their voice should be heard to-day, and I present to you Dr. Granville P. Conn of the medical staff.

In behalf of the medical staff, Dr. G. P. Conn accepted the gift as follows:

If it were not that I am confronted with the thought that my colleagues upon the medical and surgical staff of this hospital deserve a representation at this time far better than it is possible for me to give them, I certainly should count myself most fortunate that it is my privilege to speak to you words of welcome in our new home. In responding to the invitation of the trustees, the only language which my heart prompts me to utter this afternoon is the language of congratulation,—congratulations for the past, the present, and the future of our hospital.

The past extends over a period from October 20, 1884, to the present. Seven reports have been made, but the first covered a period of less than three months, and the treatment of only nine patients. The present includes the history of a period of a little less than seven years, and the treatment of 700 patients. The report ending January 1, 1891, as Mr. Eastman has told you, shows that during this time the hospital has received in cash $38,369.40, of which $18,563.73 has been received by the matron from the patients or from their friends, in part payment for the cost of their support while in the institution. The expenses of the hospital have been greatly increased by reason that a large amount ($8,000) has been paid for necessary repairs and heating apparatus, all of which the comfort and safety of the patients demanded; and these demands our trustees have met with commendable alacrity.

The number of deaths since the institution was opened has been sixty-nine, of which nearly eighty per cent. have been from chronic disease and violence, phthisis or consumption taking the lead in chronic disease, and railway injuries constituting the most of the deaths by reason of accident. Since the hospital was opened, the number of female patients treated has been slightly in excess of the males. Every hospital annually receives more or less cases demanding immediate attention by reason of injuries or very sudden illness. We have received since our hospital was opened about 140 such emergency cases—about one fifth of the whole number treated, or something less than two cases a month. These cases are made up from railway and other accidents, people taken violently ill on board the trains, and those found seriously ill at their rooms and with no one to care for them. Two or three have been taken from the trains who had been stricken with apoplexy, and lived but a few hours after being brought into the accident-room; while others have been brought here in a moribund state, because in their helpless and friendless condition they were in danger of freezing unless they were provided for at once.

Since our city furnished an ambulance, it has been used on an average more than once a week, though not always coming to the hospital. A general statement like the above illustrates the fact that we have not been exclusive, and taken only such cases as would promise good results; nor have we sent patients home to die as soon as it became obvious that their death was only a question of time, and therefore to remain in the hospital was a matter of care and comfort and a certainty to increase the mortuary rate. On the contrary, we have opened our doors to all, and made it a home to the homeless and a friend to the needy, and that we have not done more is because of our limited means and want of room. Of the future it may be sufficient to say, that judging by the past, and looking over the results of what good, conscientious clinical labor has been doing, we may hope, with our increased and improved facilities, to perform more and better work. History informs us that the original idea of a hospital was to establish places to give shelter and food to the sick poor, more especially to those who were residents of large cities : hence it was the popular notion that hospitals could only be found at populous centres. Gradually, however, physicians found they could obtain, by close observation of these aggregations of human suffering, much real information that afforded the means of teaching others; but this last use of them is only two hundred years old.

This transition of hospital work was very gradual, and in time it also came to be known that the knowledge thus obtained in the care of the sick poor was of use in treating the diseases of those in more affluent circumstances: and finally, within the last twenty-five years or so, people are beginning to find out that when they are afflicted with certain forms of disease or injury, they can be better treated in a properly appointed hospital than they can be in their own homes, no matter how costly or how luxurious these may be.

In the hospital they can have not only all the comforts of a home, but more; not only skilled medical attendance and skilled nursing, but the use of many appliances and arrangements specially devised for the comfort and welfare of the sick, which can hardly be found in any private house, and also freedom from noise and many petty annoyances,— including in some cases too much sympathy, and in others too little. I trust it is and will be our earnest wish and hope that in this hospital we shall be able at all times to care for the sick poor as well as for the affluent; for those who cannot pay, as well as for those who can and therefore ought to pay for what they receive and thus be made to assist in the support of one of the noblest charities that civilization has ever developed.

A hospital may be compared to a living organism, made up of many different parts having different functions; yet all this diversity of functional activity must be in due proportional relation to each other, as well as to the locality in which it is situated, else it will fail to produce the desired general results. The stream of life that is constantly passing through its portals is incessantly changing; patients and nurses and doctors come and go;—to-day it has to deal with the results of an epidemic; to-morrow, with those of an explosion or a fire;— this week it may be crowded with the terrible effects of a railway accident, while next week the work may be very largely confined to meeting the demands of chronic disease. The reputation of its physicians and surgeons attracts those suffering from some particular form of disease: therefore, as the one changes, so do the others.

Its work is never done; its equipment and appointments are never complete; it is always in need of new means of diagnosis, of new instruments and new medicines; it is intended to try all things, and hold fast to that which is found to be good. It aims to bring the benefits of the most advanced medical training in medical science, the most skilful nursing, and the most favoring materials and moral conditions to the relief of the suffering of all classes. It is its purpose to give a well appointed temporary home to the homeless as well as to those whose own homes lack those little appliances favorable to recovery, and adds some conditions and many appointments which the most luxurious homes cannot furnish.

I remember it has been said that "Hospitals furnish some sort of a measure of the civilization of a people." However, a hospital of this kind should be something more than a mere index; it should be an active force, a living element, in the community in which it is placed. Thus it will become a noble exponent of public charity. Having neither political, sectarian, nor socialistic ideas, it will become a benefit to all in every class that may need its help.

When the mediaeval priest established in each great city in France a Hotel Dieu, a place for God's hospitality, it was in the interest of charity as he then understood it, which included both the helping of the sick poor, as well as affording to those who were neither sick nor poor an opportunity and a stimulus to help their fellow-men; and doubtless the cause of humanity and religion was advanced more by the effect on the giver than on the receiver. And thus it comes to our minds again, the old lesson so often expounded, apparently so simple and yet so hard to learn, that true happiness lies in helping others: that it is more blessed to give than to receive.

Our fellow-citizens have nobly responded to our appeals for help during the past seven years, as one may observe by their liberal donations as reported year after year by the trustees. Men, women, and children have emulated each other in their good work in the support of an institution for the relief of suffering humanity; and, besides the amount of money that has been contributed, a great deal has been donated to support the hospital, in bedding, clothing, medicines, groceries, and other supplies,—all of which shows the tendency of the age and the spirit of the times in which we live.

These rooms, now radiant with the gracious smiles of approving friends, will sooner or later become the arena in which scientific method and observation shall be made to do their best work in relieving human suffering, and, possibly, in prolonging life. Can there be any higher aim, or a more lofty ambition to which the mind of man should strive to attain? or can a building be erected and dedicated to a purpose that will more nearly touch the hearts of the people?

The importance of such labor is second to none other, for with the production of trained investigators, full of enthusiasm and thoroughly imbued with the spirit of scientific research, the influence of its work will be far reaching. It is to the young men thus fitted for the work that we must look for the solution of some of the myriad problems which now confront the biologist and the physician. Do I seem to ask too much?—to be too sanguine as to what human thought, study, and skill may accomplish?—to forget that there is one event unto all—that the shadow of pain and death comes on the wise man as on the fool?

I would answer, that so surely as our improved methods of prevention and treatment, based on the advances in knowledge of the last fifty years, have extended the average duration of life in civilized countries nearly five years; have prolonged thousands of useful and productive lives; and have done away with the indescribable agonies of the pre-anaesthetic period,—so we are on the verge of still greater advances, especially in the prevention of infectious and contagious diseases, in the resources of surgery against deformities and morbid growths, as well as in the mitigation of suffering due to causes which cannot be wholly removed.

This epoch in medicine and surgery is more brilliant and eventful than any that has preceded it, and the prospect grows more and more encouraging with each succeeding year, and richer in its probabilities and possibilities in order to meet the expectation of popular opinion.

As medical men, we are living in an age of great

progress, and it is no longer a strife of sects or creeds, but a great struggle for intellectual supremacy over weakness and charlatanism. Superstition, bigotry, and ignorance should not for a moment be allowed a place in any man's heart, but let sound reasoning, conservatism, and good judgment be made to govern all things.

The effect of many enthusiastic co-workers in the field of science, all struggling for truth in medicine and the advancement of surgery, cannot fail to show good results, notwithstanding there are always some who are ever ready to accept an assertion for a fact, an abstraction for a reality, a glittering generalization for scientific truth. Such people are never quite satisfied with the modest representations of philosophical reasoning, and consequently are suspicious of the physician having a reputation to sustain because of his being a man of deeds rather than of high sounding words.

Dr. John W. Draper, of New York, once said, "There has been through all ages constantly hovering about honest workers in our science a host of impostors and empirical men, who will continue to thrive so long as there are weak-minded and shallow men to delude, and vain, silly women to believe;" and yet this is no better, nor is it any worse, than we may find or that may be said of all other departments of scientific research.

Religion may have its fanatics, law may have its pettifoggers, and medicine may have its pretenders, still the great principles involved in all these professions will be in no wise changed: they will ever remain the same, and the honest seeker after truth need not be discouraged on account of the seeming heresies that abound on the surface. It is true, these may appear quite dazzling when they first appeal to the senses, yet how soon their tinsel becomes tarnished when exposed to the bright sunlight of everlasting truth, or when compared with the observations of the mind governed by scientific reasoning!

I suspect it is not altogether an evil that people do not all think alike, for the discussions that grow out of honest differences of opinion may be fruitful sources of mental acumen. Hospital work, like other associate and closely united labor, will always accomplish results that would be unattainable by personal effort alone. This constant association of the medical and surgical staff has its advantages, for minds, like metals, cannot come in contact with each other without receiving some form of an impression; the more forcible the contact, the more vividly the imprint will appear.

Mental attrition develops all the latent power of the brain, sharpens every faculty, and quickens the understanding; therefore comprehension and perception are improved, questions that seem to involve principles once dim and misty become bright and clear, the outlook is broadened, the possibilities expand, and superstition and intolerance find little or no sympathy with a corps of men educated in medicine and whose training has been in the wards of a well appointed hospital.

I congratulate you, fellows of the medical and surgical staff, that, as workers in every department of scientific medicine, we meet this afternoon about our hearth-stone in the full possession of all those faculties which are needed to render our work most efficient, and that will serve to stimulate us to still higher achievement in the future; so that we may hope that the work done in these rooms shall stand the test of scientific criticism, and thus we may hold a place in forming and crystallizing the true progress of medicine and surgery in this state.

I congratulate the profession and the public that our days of doubt and anxiety regarding a hospital building are past. Success has ceased to be a question, and the auspicious present marks the beginning of a new and enlarged career for hospital work; still, with increasing opportunities come deeper obligations. We must not rely upon our past success, for a hospital is not an automatic machine: it will not run itself, and keep pace with the progressive spirit of the age in which we live. It has been said, " No man is under obligations to the past, but all men are under bonds to the future."

We should not look backwards, but forwards; and when we in turn pass this trust to our successors, to those who in the future are to be the exponents of the lofty mission to which this building is dedicated this afternoon, it must not have suffered in our hands; but we should, by our work, see that its capacity for doing good, its sphere of influence, and its good name have grown and become wide spread under the impulse of true enthusiasm, good work, and a clear understanding of all our duties.

Yesterday we read the history of the past; to-day we make history for the future; and whether he will or no, every fellow in our number must leave his mark, his impress—be it much or little—upon the records of this hospital. Professor Loomis, of New York, once remarked, "There is no place in the broad field of scientific medical inquiry for the would-be medical man who talks of the potential power of infinitesimal abstractions and so called scholastic illusions." We must not forget that we are living in, and are a part of, an age of facts, not fancies; of work, not theories.

Every hospital corps should always keep these facts in mind; and every board of officials should bear in mind, that, while dealing with funds for the purposes of charity, they should be governed by true business principles, and that business methods should underlie every action; that neither waste nor extravagance should be tolerated, any more than they would be in the ordinary commercial transactions of the counting-room. In this way we may hope to merit the full confidence of the public; and then I have faith that funds will be provided to keep this hospital equipped with every appointment necessary to enable the medical staff to accomplish all that rational medicine has or will suggest.

It is said that Johns Hopkins, of Baltimore, when asked by an intimate friend of about his own age why he had never made a will, replied that he looked upon his wealth as a gift for which he was accountable; that it grew and piled up from a small beginning, he hardly knew how; but he was sure it was given him for a purpose, and he did not believe he should die before he was given to see how he should dispose of his estate. "This wealth," he repeated, "is my stewardship." How he disposed of it; how he was given to see in what manner he should leave his immense wealth so that it should do the most good and incidentally become a distinctive mark whereby his name should become a household word throughout the land; how the institution he was the means of developing should take a front rank among the universities of this country, and be destined in the near future to be the peer, having equal educational advantages, of any of the universities of the old world,— what his reasoning might have been we may never know, except this: He called his friends about him, and, ever keeping in mind that great principle of stewardship, he rendered it possible for Baltimore to open to the world an institution which is to be so progressive in its character and so broad in all its designs that the whole United States may claim it as her own, with the same pride that Philadelphia points to that noble institution of learning that has been and will continue to be for generations to come a beautiful and a most enduring monument to the good name of Stephen Girard.

Costly paintings, monuments of stone, and statues of bronze, when compared with progressive and free institutions for the alleviation of human suffering or for educational purposes, awaken but little commendation or sentiment. The cold surface of their exterior has but little effect in developing a sympathetic and never-to-be-forgotten expression of public feeling with an intelligent people when compared with the heartfelt gratitude of some poor lad enabled to obtain a thorough education, or the praise of poverty-stricken and long-suffering humanity when relieved from physical ills and torturing pain through the influence of an institution like this, which is to be devoted to humanitarian ends.

In the dedication of this building we have the beginning of an institution which will endure long after the speakers and the audience of to-day shall have finished their life's work and have passed away; yet the name of the benefactor, whose magnificent charity has made the erection of this building possible, will be as enduring in the hearts of the people as the structure itself. In Mr. Pillsbury we have our ideal representative of a Johns Hopkins of Merrimack county, and in accepting his gift to our people the medical staff, like all other good citizens, are proud of this chance publicly to return our sincere thanks for his beneficence. As an almoner, he is able to give an account of his stewardship that few will ever attain.

The very existence of this building is the acme of a broad charity. I would congratulate him upon his successful business career, in which he has become the steward of a large bounty; and we are to be congratulated upon the evidence he has shown us that he has been "given to see" in what manner he could dispose of a part of this bounty so as to leave to Concord and New Hampshire a monument more enduring than fame, more highly prized than mere embellishments and culture, a guide to health, an emblem of the Good Samaritan. The building itself is a whole volume, a canticle of praise to the energy of its promoter, a pean of gratitude to the liberality of him whose material bounty has made its erection possible.

In behalf of my associates on the medical and surgical staff, I would again return our thanks to Mr. Pillsbury for the building which we now dedicate; and with the most sincere gratitude for the bestowal of these favors, let us pledge ourselves anew to the professional labors belonging to hospital work. In behalf of the medical profession of the state, I would return grateful thanks for this gift of a hospital, founded in the interest of suffering humanity, reared by the hand of munificent charity, dedicated to the city of Concord in particular and to the state of New Hampshire in general. It is a most beautiful tribute to a wife's devotion, a monument to a woman's affections, and indicates a just confidence in a woman's love of doing good; therefore we have every reason to predict for it a long and prosperous career, with steadily progressive improvements in its organization and methods, and an ever increasing sphere of influence, activity, and usefulness.

Following these speakers the quartette rendered a selection, after which Rev. Cephas B. Crane, D.D., offered the dedicatory prayer, which was followed by music.

His Honor Mayor Clapp spoke for the city of Concord as follows:

MR. PRESIDENT, HON. AND MRS. PILLSBURY, LADIES AND GENTLEMEN: To-day is indeed a gala one for Concord. It witnesses the final completion of one of its fondest hopes, a magnificent city hospital finished in a most satisfactory manner. It will be for years a monument to the generosity of our former citizen, Hon. George A. Pillsbury. During the years of his residence here he won for himself the highest esteem of every citizen by his philanthropic nature, his straightforward business ability, his faithful discharge of every public trust reposed in him, and especially do we remember the judicious manner in which he performed his duties as mayor of our city. His noble-heartedness, so often expressed in real acts, was recognized by all classes, and when he left us for a Western home we all felt that we had lost a personal friend as well as an honored citizen. Success has ever followed his footsteps; fortunes have been laid at his feet;—with all this abundance he has not betrayed the trust reposed in him, but unselfishness has continued to predominate. He conceived the idea of erecting a city hospital in his former New England home, and thus, by alleviating the pain and sickness to which flesh is heir, forever to perpetuate his memory in the hearts of his Concord friends. When he made known his intentions, our appreciation of such a gift could not be fully expressed. Surely we had not misplaced the high esteem which we held for him in the past, as one who had the true interests of all mankind at heart!

To-day there stands upon this site an edifice within whose walls words of praise shall rise from the lips of suffering ones long after many of us are gone who needed not this costly expression to remind us of his noble nature.

In naming this institution the Margaret Pillsbury General Hospital, Mr. Pillsbury has forever welded with his own the name of the loved companion of his earthly life, who, by her counsel and co-working, has gone hand in hand with him in all his good works. By instinct woman assumes the office of nurse for the sick and suffering; hence the name has another important significance. Furthermore, it seems to me, by erecting this hospital during the lifetime of himself and wife, he has penetrated far into the depths of unalloyed happiness in this world, and they must feel to-day that they are allowed to witness the fruits of an unselfish one—a foretaste of the hereafter. Not by all who have the heart to perform such acts as this can such joy be known;—for some, their gifts must assume form by other hands than theirs, and their works live after them in hallowed remembrance; to still others, the privilege of giving in any public way is most emphatically denied—only little deeds permitted, lost to human eyes but accounted for at the final reckoning.

We know full well that these large-hearted Christian friends of ours, Mr. and Mrs. Pillsbury, the donors of this building, will gladly share the glory of this gift with the departed ones who have made bequests to this hospital; with those who, against obstacles great in the extreme, founded it on a site just north of the present one, and have given to it ungrudgingly much of their valuable time and experience; with those who have donated sums sufficient for free beds; with those who have furnished rooms, and done smaller acts of kindness; and with our little ones, whose various ways of earning and saving their pennies are fast swelling a fund for a child's free bed: all these, I am sure, will be welcome to walk side by side with the donors of this structure, magnificent as it is, because in each instance whatever has been done has been the result of a noble purpose proportioned as each has been blessed.

As the weeks, months, and years roll by, and one and another are stricken down,—many possibly who are here in health to-day,—and receive here tender care, effective skill, and in every possible instance ultimate recovery, there will be continual expressions of gratitude toward the donors of this hospital, whose generosity has made possible a shelter in which the sick may be nursed back to health.

Dear friends, I have expressed to you, as best I can, the heartfelt thanks of every citizen, great and small, of our fair city, for this substantial evidence of your deep love and respect for them. Words are inadequate after all, and you both are enjoying to-day in realization what to but few can ever be more than anticipation. It is very evident to us all that you hold in your hands the key to real, unadulterated happiness, which you can turn at your will;—hence we can only say we rejoice with you: it has been well earned. The sunset of your lives is a gorgeously brilliant one;—that it may linger long, and continue bright, before its final fading, is the sincere wish of the people of our city.

Governor Tuttle was then presented to speak for the state. He said,—

This occasion is one of interest, not only to those of us participating in it, but it will have important and far reaching consequences upon the future well-being and happiness of the people of this prosperous and growing city.

Even as far back as the fourth century the establishment of hospitals was commenced; but it has remained for the people of this century to give prominence to the idea of establishing hospitals in the cities and large towns of the world. It is certainly an evidence of the growth of human sympathy and benevolence thus to provide by charity for the mitigation of the misfortunes of the sick and the afflicted. It is a grand work, lessening suffering and pain, and broadening and deepening the higher and nobler attributes of human nature.

Concord is surely to be congratulated upon the completion of so beautiful and well appointed a hospital. It is not only a blessing, but also an ornament to the city. While to-day it is properly regarded as a monument to the generosity of one man, in years to come it will be known as the hope of the suffering, and as an asylum for those in need of its beneficent ministrations. To it will be turned the eyes of the poor and the unfortunate, and from it will go up many prayers for him who gave it, and for her whose name it bears. Within its walls human suffering will appeal to human skill, and added health and strength will be given to the sick and the sorrowing. It is surely a great gift: it is infinitely better than monuments of marble or of bronze, for while they will crumble and decay, the charities and benefactions of this place will live in the memory of our people long after the donor has passed away.

For many years I have known Mr. Pillsbury, and to him I am personally indebted for friendly aid and advice. No man in the state has watched his career with greater interest than I, or rejoiced more over his prosperity both here and in Minnesota. He is truly a good man, wearing his honors meekly, and dispensing his benefactions with an open hand. Surely it is a great privilege to join in the tribute of appreciation that the people of Concord so gladly render to their former townsman and their constant friend.

Mr. Chairman, projecting myself into the future, I can see in dim outline the great work of benevolence that is to be wrought out in this institution. Here suffering will be relieved, sorrow mitigated, discouragement overcome, tears dried, and hopes revived. All through the years its mission will go on, and all through the years the mind that planned and the heart that executed this great undertaking will, if permitted to look upon the scenes of this world after his life-work is done, be cheered by the results of his generous gift.

I can do no more than express the hope that for many long years to come Mr. and Mrs. Pillsbury may live to witness the successful workings of the hospital now being dedicated; and I know that future generations will speak their names gratefully and reverently, because of the liberality of their hearts in founding this noble charity. God bless them both.

Senator William E. Chandler was presented as a representative of those who had contributed to the hospital, and spoke thus:

By three recent acts of benevolence in New Hampshire, Mr. Pillsbury has expressed for himself, and aroused in others, sentiments in the highest degree characteristic of the communities where he was born and reared and achieved his first successes in life, and of which he is one of the finest products and representatives.

By erecting a monument in Sutton, the home of his birth, to commemorate the life and death of those soldiers of the town who went out from her rural valleys to fight the battles of the Union, he has invoked the noble sentiment of patriotism. If it is sweet and becoming to die for one's country, how grand were the sacrifices made by those patriots who left their homes and families to surrender their lives in the holiest war ever waged on earth. Begun to save the first true and great republic of the world from the deadly assaults of the slaveholders of the South, who were making merchandise of human souls and seeking to dissolve the Union because the North would yield no more territory to be cursed by the sum of all villanies, it ended in the utter destruction of that crime against God and nature, and it saved, strengthened, and made more glorious and precious than ever the incomparable republic of the United States. But, for the salvation of the nation and the destruction of slavery, of 2,225,000 soldiers enlisted, 110,000 were slain in battle, and 360,000 in all gave up their lives for the preservation of the government and for the liberation of a race. Surely he who builds a monument to remind the men of to-day and to teach their children of the great price which between 1860 and 1865 the Union soldiers paid to save, through civil war, the nation which was founded by the blood of the soldiers of 1776, has wisely expended his resources, and is entitled to the gratitude of every patriotic American heart.

By giving a free public library to Warner, the home of Mr. Pillsbury's early manhood, he has recognized a sentiment which, if not so emotional as some others, has perhaps as much real strength as any, because, as much as any other, it is founded on the deepest convictions of the nation. Without education for the whole people a republic cannot live, and the maintenance of the broadest popular education is everywhere conceded to be one of the indispensable requisites for the perpetuity of our free institutions. If any one doubts whether our devotion to popular education is a deep and powerful sentiment, let him for a moment imagine the consequences of any assault which might appear likely to be successful upon the common schools of America. The universal tumult which would arise would fearfully startle the enemies of the system, and drive them into hasty retreat. In the presence of no immediate danger, the sentiment which sustains our public schools may be slumbering; but let those who, for any reason whatever, fancy they may substitute for them something better, beware of making the attempt. They will rouse the whirlwind and will reap the storm.

A growing adjunct to our public schools are the free libraries. Increased knowledge among men demands greater facilities for its diffusion. The zeal for learning acquired by scholars will not be satisfied with school text-books nor with books kept in private libraries, and the demand for wider means of knowledge must be met. Wherever in our large American towns the primary and grammar schools are complete, there will be good high schools; and soon there surely comes a free public library. The children of one of our best known citizens have generously given to Concord the Fowler Public Library. Mr. Pillsbury has given a free public library to Warner. By these libraries is the sentiment of devotion to popular education as the foundation stone of the republic exemplified and strengthened in the hearts of all wise and good citizens.

But a sentiment probably the most tender which human beings ever feel is that which has given to the city of Concord the Margaret Pillsbury General Hospital, and which causes the gift to be so joyously welcomed by this whole people. Sympathy for physical suffering and the desire to alleviate bodily anguish constitute, doubtless, the most universal and impulsive sentiment which prevails among highly civilized races like our own. Nowhere, I think I may claim, is there to be more abundantly found the unwillingness to inflict physical pain and the wish to relieve and cure it than in New England. Cruelty to animals and men is a part of the sports of some nations; less do such brutal feelings exist in America than anywhere else, and in New Hampshire they find no place whatever. Human life is held highly sacred, and pain and sickness are regarded as evils which the whole community should make haste to remove. This feeling is not merely characteristic of a high order of civilization, but it is founded upon deep religious sentiment.

Jesus of Nazareth went about in all Galilee, "healing all manner of disease and all manner of sickness among the people." "They brought unto him all that were sick, holden with divers diseases and torments, and he healed them." To his disciples he gave authority "to heal all manner of disease and all manner of sickness." When John the Baptist sent word, and asked, "Art thou he that cometh?" he replied, "Go your way, and tell John what things ye have seen and heard: the blind receive their sight, the lame walk, the lepers are cleansed, and the deaf hear;" and then, and not till then, when grievous sickness, agonizing bodily suffering, and oppressive physical infirmities were removed, was the gospel preached unto the poor of this world.

That the desire to heal sickness and relieve physical pain is the strongest and tenderest sentiment of human nature is proved by the constant association of woman with hospital work. Man is supposed always to reason before acting; woman is quick to feel, and act on instinct, and to rush on impulse to the help of the sick, the suffering, and the dying. Mr. Pillsbury appropriately associates with this hospital the name of his wife. It would not be natural to so link her name with a soldiers' monument; it would not be so natural to connect it with a public library; but it is most fitting that with this supreme benefaction of his in New Hampshire,—a hospital for the proper care and cure of sick and suffering humanity,—the memory of a good woman should be perpetuated. The work is crowned by the name of his wife, and will forever stand a glory to the sex which, following the footsteps of the Redeemer and aiding him in his double work of curing the bodies and saving the souls of men, was found "last at the cross and earliest at the grave."

So here and now, Concord has her Margaret Pillsbury General Hospital. The proper modern treatment of many diseases, the best method of managing surgical cases, require such a structure. Perfect in all its appointments, admirably adapted in every way to the wants of the city and the state, the gratitude of this community to the generous donor is fully and formally expressed by the appropriate ceremonies of this hour.

I have been requested to speak for the contributors who have aided in fitting the building for use. These are substantially the persons who aided in establishing the hospital which this new edifice is to replace. Seven years ago, realizing the need of such an institution, they went forward doing what they could and trusting to the future. Humble in its beginnings, the hospital was from time to time enlarged and improved. Unexpected contributions came in. Some of those who gave to the enterprise liberally of their labor and money have gone to their reward. Many are here to-day. The work grew and prospered, and is a just testimony to the fidelity and humanity of its projectors.

For these contributors to the old hospital I set up the claim that to them as well as to Mr. Pillsbury this community owes this new edifice. The Lord helps those who help themselves. I cannot doubt that Mr. Pillsbury's attention was attracted to the need of a better hospital in Concord by the fact that there already existed here a fairly good one in successful operation. He saw the efforts that were being made by the men and women of this growing community to meet the imperative demand for a public institution where persons suddenly stricken down by accident could be carried; where medical and surgical emergencies could be met; where certain diseases could be treated and certain modes of treatment adopted not possible in private houses; and where the poor in this world's goods, critically diseased, could receive proper care and attendance;—and seeing his Concord friends doing so much by their benevolent labors and with their own resources to sustain a hospital necessary and creditable to the city, he was impelled to come over and help them. I know nothing of the facts, but I have no doubt that it would be safe to appeal to Mr. Pillsbury to say that because he saw us doing so much and so well, there came to him a strong and irresistible desire to help us do more and better; and that he most probably would not have been led to give us this grand hospital if there had been none here before.

At all events, I think that the greatest lesson to be taken to heart to-day is this,—that after all, the chief value of this hospital is not what it now is, but what it shall be hereafter made by the men and women of Concord. That which costs nothing is apt to be undervalued, and not to be sufficiently cared for and properly used. I know a religious society whose church edifice has been wholly given to it, and also liberal endowments for its support, which is by no means a flourishing society. It languishes, and it is not a desirable organization to be connected with. The spirit of self-help is gone, and with it have departed zeal and effort, prosperity and success.

Such a result of the gift of this hospital must be avoided. The people of Concord must gratefully accept this building exactly as it is given to them, as a sacred trust which must be supplemented by exertions of their own. They must raise money for it, visit it, guard it, improve it, and strive to make it a model hospital for the world to look at and imitate. Do not forget that it was Mr. Pillsbury's, but do not fail to realize that it is now your own. He gives it to you, and goes away from it to his Western home. It is given to you ungrudgingly, and you cannot take too firm a hold of it to suit him; but it is given to be cared for and used, and not to be neglected. It should be made a great blessing to our city and to the state, a credit to Concord as well as to its benevolent donor.

To you, sir, and to your beloved wife I think I may make this promise: that the people of Concord,—those who have known you personally as one of our citizens; those younger men and women who know you by your acts of wise benevolence; and those who are to come upon the stage after we all are gone,—will guard and protect and improve and develop this humane institution in accordance with your wishes, as long as the city stands, making it a glowing illustration of the tenderest sentiments of which the human heart is capable, and an imperishable memorial of the noble name it bears.

A benediction by Rev. Dr. Crane closed the exercises. The orchestra played several selections while the audience were inspecting the building.

RECEPTION AND BANQUET, FOLLOWING DEDICATORY EXERCISES.

In the evening a reception and banquet were tendered Hon. and Mrs. George A. Pillsbury by the city of Concord, at the New Eagle hotel. The municipal and citizens' committee having the affair in charge were Mayor Clapp, Aldermen Woodworth and Sanders, Councilmen Crowell, Nutter, and Cloudman, Hon. B. A. Kimball, Hon. William M. Chase, Samuel S. Kimball, Esq., Joseph B. Walker, Esq., Rev. C. B. Crane, D. D., Col. Charles C. Danforth, and N. E. Martin, Esq. The reception began at 7:30 o'clock in the parlor of the hotel, the receiving party consisting of Mr. and Mrs. Pillsbury, Governor and Mrs. Tuttle, Mayor and Mrs. Clapp, Mrs. Frank S. Streeter, Mrs. Lyman D. Stevens, Mrs. Edson C. Eastman, Mrs. Elizabeth P. Schütz, and Dr. Julia Wallace-Russell. The ushers were Col. Frank W. Rollins, Paul R. Holden, H. Gordon Hutchins, Frank P. Andrews, Alderman George F. Underhill, and Henry W. Stevens, Esq. The reception and banquet committee were Mayor Clapp, Alderman E. B. Woodworth, and Col. Charles C. Danforth.

For more than an hour a line of representative men and women of the city surged through the parlors to pay their respects to the benefactors of the city, and extend to them their kindest wishes. Blaisdell's orchestra, stationed in the hall, played several charming selections during the reception, and also during the banquet which followed. The parlors were decorated with cut flowers, smilax, potted plants, and palms, and the scene was a brilliant and most enjoyable one.

A few minutes before 9 o'clock, to the music of a march by the orchestra, the guests proceeded to the dining-hall, where plates had been laid for two hundred persons, and all were taken. The apartment presented a beautiful appearance, the tables being decorated with smilax and palms. At each plate was a handsome boutonnière.

The menu card was a handsome four-page folder, bearing on the front of its cover a neat photogravure of the Margaret Pillsbury General Hospital, and the words "Complimentary Banquet to Mr. and Mrs. George A. Pillsbury, by the City of Concord, N. H., on the occasion of the dedication of the Margaret Pillsbury General Hospital, Monday, October 5, 1891. At the New Eagle Hotel."

After grace had been said by Very Rev. J. E. Barry, V. G., the attention of the company was devoted to the banquet, which was pronounced by all present to be the finest ever served in the city. It occupied an hour and a half, and it was 10:15 o'clock when Mayor Clapp rapped the company to order and said,—

LADIES AND GENTLEMEN: Will you please come to order.

The gratefulness of the citizens of Concord towards Hon. and Mrs. George A. Pillsbury for their munificent gift has been forcibly demonstrated by the many who have availed themselves of this public reception to take them by the hand, and in a more feeling way express to them what I attempted to do in words this afternoon at the dedication of the Margaret Pillsbury General Hospital. All the preparations for this event have been entered into heart and soul by the committee, feeling that the most that could be done was little indeed. These preparations have met the hearty approval of the people, affording them the opportunity and pleasure of meeting our distinguished guests in person. This reception and banquet seem an appropriate ending of this eventful day.

It now gives me great pleasure to introduce to you one of our ablest and most respected physicians, Dr. F. A. Stillings, who will have charge of the post-prandial exercises of the evening.

On assuming the duties of his position, Dr. Stillings said,—

LADIES AND GENTLEMEN: Why His Honor the Mayor thrust this duty upon me I was at first unable to tell, but I have come to the conclusion that he wanted some one to preside at this dinner who could not possibly make a speech if he tried to. In fact, he privately gives me to understand that I am simply to press the button and you will do the rest.

It has been said, the good that men do "is oft interred with their bones." We have met to-night to do honor to a man and a woman who have done good that will not die with them, but live for all time,—

The Hon. George A. Pillsbury and his wife Margaret Sprague Pillsbury.

As Mr. Pillsbury arose he was received with tumultuous applause, which died away only to be renewed again. He received an ovation, and was compelled to bow his acknowledgments for several minutes before he could be heard. He said,—

I supposed I was to respond to a toast, but as you have given me no sentiment, I do not know just what to say. I have been thinking, though, since I came here, that so much praise as we have received is likely to make trouble. Mine is a beautiful wife to live with, but I am afraid that so much praise will affect her so that she will dictate to me more than ever. She joins me in expressing thanks for the honor you have done us. I believe in the Scriptures, and they say that it is more blessed to give than to receive; but we have received so many kind wishes, that we feel that the rule is in great danger of reversal.

It is very pleasant for us to be here, and to meet so many associates of the years past, whom we were permitted to know when we lived here. It does us good to look into the faces of so many old-time friends to-night. I read the Concord papers, and it seems that hardly a week goes by without our learning of the death of some former friend. But many yet remain, and we are thankful for it.

We have never had anything but respect and love and esteem for the people of Concord, and these feelings are enhanced by meeting you on this occasion. We know that you appreciate the little we have done, and we shall ever remember your kind words and cordial greetings. We hope to visit Concord often. It is a pleasure to meet you all, and we hope that our lives may be spared to greet you many times again. Let us all try to make the world better for our having lived in it.

Dr. Stillings. I now have the pleasure of introducing Dr. S. C. Morrill, who will speak for

The Margaret Pillsbury General Hospital and its Medical Staff.

Dr. Morrill said,—

The Margaret Pillsbury General Hospital is by far the largest, by far the most useful, and by far the most Christian gift ever offered to the city of Concord.

In regard to the men who are an indispensable part of the belongings of all institutions of this sort, viz., the medical staff of the Margaret Pillsbury General Hospital, it must first of all be understood that I am not an impartial nor unprejudiced witness. This staff claims to have done much good work during seven long years in the "great pill" hospital. It hopes to prove itself equal to the task of extending its work, in proportion to the improved facilities and accommodations the new building will offer it.

In this connection it is perhaps not seriously betraying confidence to say that the present staff is waiting, if not working, for some silk-worm transformation into a double staff, one part being skilled mechanics, alias surgeons, who with a formidable array of tools complacently saw off your legs and arms, and the other part being skilled artisans, alias physicians, who with pills and powders, blisters and hypodermics, annihilate pain and fever, and give peaceful sleep to hyper-aesthetic brains. Whether this desirable transformation be accomplished or not, I am sure the Margaret Pillsbury Hospital ought, and will, inspire its medical staff to devote itself at all times to the one effort of making this the most beneficent institution in the state.

Gentlemen of the medical staff, let us pledge ourselves to imitate our benefactor, who, "having decided to be a philanthropist, immediately formed a plan and began the execution of it without delay, proceeding to do something which obliged him to do more—something which imposed upon him the necessity of doing all." Let us shout in admiration of our guest, who, seeing that life is no more than a day between two Arctic nights, hastens here and elsewhere to comfort the sick and to silence the discordant voices of ignorance. Let us offer good cheer to the man who gives the solace of good nursing to our fellow-citizens who lie in the shadow of death! Let us drink to the health of the man who offers shelter, wholesome food, invigorating air and light, to those convalescents who impatiently wait for strength to take up their customary work!

Dr. STILLINGS. The beneficence of the Margaret Pillsbury Hospital is not confined to this city and its vicinity, but is far reaching, and to reply for

The State of New Hampshire,

I present to you His Excellency the Governor.

Governor Tuttle responded as follows:

Mr. Toast-Master, Ladies and Gentlemen: I thank the gentlemen of the committee for the privilege of being here to-night with the citizens of Concord, assembled to signify their appreciation of the gift they have this day received from two former residents, who, although they now have their home and business in the great Western state of Minnesota, have never ceased to remember and cherish a love for the state of their nativity, and for the city where they lived so many years.

Mr. Pillsbury was one of my first acquaintances when I came to Concord, more than thirty years ago; and wherever I have met him, in his beautiful Western home or occasionally on his visits to the East, I have found him the same kind, noble-hearted Christian gentleman, who always had a cheering word for the poor boy so many years ago. The increase of wealth, the cares of business, and great prosperity have not changed the man and woman who went from your midst, save that with an increase of wealth they have been able to do more for their fellow-men. Through all these years they have been ardent supporters of all that is good and noble; and it has ever been in the hearts of Mr. Pillsbury and his good wife to give of their abundance for the comfort of those who have been less fortunate than they.

That they should feel to do what they have in erecting such a beautiful building within your limits must be a matter of pride not only to the city which it ornaments, but to the whole state. It is pleasant also to remember that not only has Concord been especially favored, but that in other places they have erected lasting monuments of their generosity. Surely Mr. and Mrs. Pillsbury must feel that it is more blessed to give than to receive. As the chief executive, I can say that New Hampshire feels honored to-day by this gift to her capital city.

DR. STILLINGS. I now propose the sentiment,

The Old-time Acquaintances of Mr. and Mrs. Pillsbury,

and call upon the friend of a half century, boyhood and manhood, Mr. John M. Hill.

Mr. Hill said,—

I respond to your call, Mr. President, with a few brief words, as I should be derelict in duty did I fail to do so.

In my early life, at the age of eighteen, I became associated in the publication in this city of a weekly and a monthly newspaper, and my friend, Mr. Pillsbury, then a young merchant in the town of Warner, assisted largely in extending the circulation, and in the general promotion, of these journals. It brought us occasionally in pleasant connection, which was enhanced by a more frequent personal intercourse, and by other and closer business relations after he came to Concord; and this has been supplemented by a continuous exchange of written and printed postal matter during his residence in the West. From a knowledge thus obtained, covering a period of a full half century of intimacy, I can well estimate the generous impulses of his nature, always prominent in his strong and broad and genial characte., and which have found expression at all periods of his life and in every vicissitude of his fortune.

In the general acclaim, it would seem almost a work of supererogation to speak of his last act towards us. Words fail to express adequately our appreciation of th's princely establishment of the greatest of human charities. It rests in the hearts of all men and women in this community, and future years will successively add to its force. The memorial will stand, a monument of noble philanthropy, and generations will arise after us to honor the good names and the fame of its founders.

I would bespeak for my friend and his estimable

wife a safe return to their Western home, and may the blessing of God be with them.

DR. STILLINGS. There are officers who have been connected with hospitals since hospitals were first known. They are modest, kindly martyrs, willing to work for the good of others without recompense, and, besides, are of great service to the doctors, who when anything goes wrong can always lay it to the trustees. I take pleasure in introducing to you one of

Our Trustees,

who has served regularly since our hospital first started, Mr. J. C. A. Hill.

Mr. Hill spoke of his pleasant connection with the hospital from its commencement, and of the good that had been accomplished by it for the sick and suffering in this city and vicinity; of its small beginning and increased usefulness year by year; of its now largely increased facilities for treatment of the sick and injured through the munificence of the donors of the Margaret Pillsbury Hospital, whose beautiful portraits we had seen suspended upon the walls of the hospital to-day; and, in closing, he thanked the donors for the added gift of their portraits.

DR. STILLINGS. As the gentleman I am about to call upon is not accustomed to speak in public, I have spent a good deal of time trying to get an easy subject for him. I give him

The Motive of a Hospital,

and present to you the Rev. Dr. D. C. Roberts.

Rev. Dr. Roberts responded in a gem of a speech, sparkling with wit and wisdom, and polished with eloquence.

DR. STILLINGS. There are certain workers connected with every hospital, to whose untiring and unselfish efforts is due much of the good reputation any hospital gains. I present to you Dr. Charles R. Walker, who will speak for

The Hospital Nurse.

Dr. Walker responded as follows:

MR. TOASTMASTER, LADIES AND GENTLEMEN: I deem it indeed an honor and a privilege to respond on this memorable occasion to the toast just given, The Hospital Nurse.

Thanks to the beneficence of noble men and women, hospitals are being founded all over our country for the alleviation of suffering. With each institution, as a part of its useful work, is established a training-school for nurses. The days of the Sairey Gamps are numbered, and we shall surely see in the near future her place taken by the bright, intelligent, well posted women who are yearly graduated from our hospitals. What the manager is to a business corporation, what the executive officer is to a ship, the skilled nurse is to your household, when one of its members lies stricken by disease, and a life hangs by a thread so slender that only her skilful attention to every detail prevents its breaking. None but physicians realize what disastrous results in sickness are often due to mistaken kindness. It is the experience gained from systematic instruction and the care of numberless cases that makes our hospital nurses so invaluable.

But I should be remiss did I not express the personal gratitude of our own hospital nurses to Mr. and Mrs. Pillsbury. Their generous gift means to the nurses palatial rooms, and many comforts unknown in the old building. Not only that, but by the increased size of the hospital many more young women can be received into the training-school, and be given an education that will enable them readily to conquer in their battle of life.

Sooner or later we shall all need the helping hand of these same trained nurses. Then, as never before, shall we realize their true value. Then shall we feel, as perhaps we do not now, the value, to us personally, through them, of this noble charity, the Margaret Pillsbury Hospital and its training-school for nurses. I know, therefore, you will all desire to join in the heartfelt wish of the hospital nurse, that the day may be far, far distant when the services of any of her sisters shall be needed in the home of that noble husband and wife, the Hon. and Mrs. George A. Pillsbury.

DR. STILLINGS. I have one more sentiment to offer,

The City of Concord and its Benevolent Institutions.

May they do as good work in the future as they have done in the past! I have the honor to name one who needs no introduction to you, Mr. Henry J. Crippen.

Mr. Crippen said,—

In assigning to me The City of Concord and its Benevolent Institutions, I presume it was not expected that I would dwell at any length upon the great charity which is the cause of our assembling here to-night, but, rather, that I would bring to public notice those minor, but perhaps not less useful, charities in which our city abounds. Few know their number, and I doubt if any one individual can name them all, and yet they are daily ministering to suffering and relieving distress of which the public never knows.

Concord has been fortunate in her children who have left her. Absence, instead of diminishing, seems to increase their love, and they return to manifest their affection by their deeds. For all of our prominent public benefactions,—the Rolfe and Rumford Asylum, the Fowler Library, and the Margaret Pillsbury Hospital,—we are indebted to those who once were residents of Concord but had ceased to be so before their gifts were made. There seems to be something in the air of Concord that will germinate but not develop the seeds of generosity, and it is necessary to transplant them for a time to distant states or to foreign lands to insure a vigorous and fruitful growth.

Probably some of our present residents contemplate endearing their memory to their fellow-citizens by similar acts of beneficence, but are waiting till they shall have reached "The undiscovered country, from whose bourn no traveller returns," and to which they can carry none of their earthly possessions.

Doubtless our friend, to whom we are indebted for the Margaret Pillsbury Hospital, feels much more satisfaction in knowing that his generous intentions are carried out, and seeing in his lifetime something of the good that he has done, than he would in thinking that he had made provision for the same objects in his will.

When we consider the uncertainty about the intentions of a testator being fulfilled, and the great probability that the lawyers instead of the legatees will be the chief beneficiaries of a will in which much is bequeathed for public purposes, it behooves us to be the almoners of our own bounty, and not trust too much to the uncertain decisions of the courts or to the acquiescence of expectant heirs.

Few of us can, either while living or at death, endow asylums, establish libraries, or build hospitals. Our contributions for charity must be united with those of others in order to be of much use. It is these small contributions of the many that support the minor charitable organizations to which I have alluded. Every church and every secret society has its own, designed especially to aid the members of the body with which it is connected. There are others, whose membership and work are confined to no sect, society, or nationality. The active workers are women, who go to the homes of the needy, relieve their necessities, nurse their sick, and by their assistance frequently enable the wage-earner of the family to continue at his ordinary occupation. By their timely ministrations many cases of sickness that would otherwise become serious are checked in their beginning, and the demands upon the hospital are thus diminished. The worthy poor, who would shrink from receiving aid from the city, accept assistance from those women as from friends, and many, who having once accepted public charity would be chronic applicants for it thereafter, preserve their self-respect, and continue to be self-supporting. The small amount of suffering and poverty in our city is largely due to the work of these societies, and yet it is done so quietly that we do not realize that it is done at all. None know the amount of good they do. The hospital itself owes its origin to them. A few winters ago a young girl was sick in a room adjoining the family kitchen, and all the warmth her room could receive came through the open door, with the odors and noise that are inseparable from a kitchen. Her friends were too poor to furnish suitable care or nourishment. Some members of one of these societies heard of her case. They cared for her, and provided everything that was necessary, and she recovered; but the difficulty of treating a case of sickness under such circumstances was so impressed on their minds and that of the attending physician, that they decided to procure some place to which the sick, who could not receive proper care at home, might be taken.

Dr. S. C. Morrill started a subscription, and in a short time money enough was pledged to support a hospital for two years, and in the following autumn the Concord Hospital was opened. The establishment of the hospital does not remove the necessity for continuing to support those charitable societies. There is work enough for both, and in different fields.

One, only, of our secret societies, the Odd Fellows, has erected a home for its needy members. Another charitable organization, which, though it has been quite liberally remembered by a few, is still largely dependent for its support on the contributions of the many, affords a home to aged people, so far as it has capacity to receive them. Its old building is so dilapidated and so insufficient that a new and larger one is an imperative necessity. It has been commenced, but funds are not provided for its completion. The Centennial Home for the Aged is a worthy object for any one who is disposed to emulate the generosity of the giver of the Margaret Pillsbury Hospital.

Concord's charities in their variety seem to embrace all classes and conditions. The orphan asylums give homes to the young and friendless; the churches, secret societies, and general benevolent associations relieve those who can be aided at their homes; the Odd Fellows' Home and the Home for the Aged offer to those who have outlived their family and friends a place where their few remaining days may be passed in comfort; and the hospital furnishes to the sick, without regard to age, sect, or social position, all the advantages which the best nursing and medical skill of our city can afford.

Our varied charities seem to provide for all. The question is asked, "Will they be as useful in the future?" Why should they not be? All are better equipped for their work to-day than they have ever been before; and, as our city increases in population, there is more work for them to do. Some of them are now in pressing need of funds, and all could use more money to advantage if they had it. The answer to the question depends largely upon ourselves. If we provide the means, Concord's charities will be more useful in the future than they have been in the past.

Dr. Stillings: Ladies and gentlemen, this closes the speaking for this evening; but as you go out from here to your several duties, I trust you will all keep alive *A Kindly Interest for the Margaret Pillsbury Hospital and its Donors.*

www.ingramcontent.com/pod-product-compliance
Lightning Source LLC
Chambersburg PA
CBHW020906230426
43666CB00008B/1326